Veritas Publication
Copyright © 2020 All Right Reserved.

No part of this publication may be reproduced, distributed, or transmitted in any form or by any means, including photocopying, recording, scanning, or other electronic or mechanical methods, or by any information storage and retrieval system, without the prior written permission of the publisher, author, or the assigned legal representative, except as permitted under Section 107 or 108 of the 1976 US Copyright Act.

Request for use should be sent direct to; veritaspublication@outlook.com.

ISBN: 978-0-578-64214-7

Table of Contents

Chapter 01 - Cold Love………………………...	Page 001
Chapter 02 – Relationships…………………….	Page 004
Chapter 03 - Cold Love, A Facet of Love…………..	Page 007
Chapter 04 - Exploring Your Inner Self…………….	Page 012
Chapter 05 - We the Victims………………………..	Page 020
Chapter 06 - Fueling the Fire………………………	Page 026
Chapter 07 - Cold Love vs Emotional Intelligence...	Page 030
Chapter 08 - Sense & Emotion…………………….	Page 033
Chapter 09 - Circumstantial Insight………………	Page 037
Chapter 10 - Tolerance of Abuse or Exploitation...	Page 040
Chapter 11 - Our Inner Rage……………………...	Page 047
Chapter 12 - Self Exploration……………………...	Page 053
Chapter 13 - Do We Need Cold Love……………..	Page 060
Chapter 14 - Indicators of Cold Love…………….	Page 064
Chapter 15 - How do we end Cold Love…………..	Page 067
Chapter 16 - Understanding Emotional Pain……..	Page 072
Chapter 17 - Responsibilities in a Relationship…..	Page 078
Chapter 18 - The White Knight Syndrome……….	Page 084
Chapter 19 - The Burning Hate Inside……………	Page 090
Chapter 20 - Question Yourself……………………	Page 096
Chapter 21 - Cold Love's Fallout…………………	Page 101
Chapter 22 - Seeking our Heaven on Earth………	Page 107
Chapter 23 - Risk and Reward…………………….	Page 111
Chapter 24 - The Foundations for Cold Love…….	Page 116
Chapter 25 - Truth or Moral Credentialing………	Page 122
Chapter 26 - Cold Love Seeds Resentment……….	Page 125
Chapter 27 - Cold Love is Fickle…………………..	Page 132
Chapter 28 - Cold Love Thrives in Narcissism…...	Page 137
Chapter 29 - Cold Love Destroys Self-Esteem……	Page 146
Chapter 30 - Falling Out of Love………………….	Page 151
Chapter 31: Love & Cold Love, Evolves………….	Page 158
Closing………………………………………………	Page 165
Glossary…………………………………………….	Page 166

Dedication

I present this composition of findings to all of the couples, and single persons, who opened up to me and shared their innermost intimate thoughts. As they expressed their fears and desires about their relationships, past and present, we came to know each other closer than a best friend could hope.

All parties involved in the decades of research and counseling sessions understood that my ultimate quest was to explore the many perceptions, opinions, and beliefs on humanity's interpretation of what we call Love.

Their names may never be known, but it is my hope that the insight derived from the past 40 years of analysis may go on to serve the greater good.

I also dedicate this book to the person(s) now reading it. If the insight contained herein allows you to better understand what Cold Love is and how it affects your life and relationships, then my life-long effort will account for something positive. I thank each of you for the privilege!

Introduction

No matter where you are on this entire planet Earth you will find people who think they can define LOVE in just a few words. Terms like "warm", "pure", "kind", "fulfilling", and many-many others. However, their answer may vary greatly depending on what type of relationship is involved, it's duration, it's type, and at what stage. Within the early stages of a relationship, LOVE may first appear to be all of the positive adjectives above, but often what we once called LOVE may begin to take on different meanings as that same love appears to change, dampen, or even go down a darker path. Did that LOVE you once considered to be so pure truly go bad, or did your perception of that LOVE change? This is just one of the reasons behind this extended study of "Cold Love", to address our understandings of what we think love is or should be.

The study of Natural Sciences states that the Universe speaks to us in numbers, not a singular ruling, so why would Love be any less complicated. Love is not a single-sided emotion as common lore would have us to believe. Love is not merely a conclusion of either yes or no, black or white. Love has many meanings and plains of interpretation, more similar to the facets on a diamond or a sphere, and as many definitions as there are opinions from the masses.

Try to imagine Love as a multi-faceted spectrum, with a multitude of viewpoints. In a simplistic form, we could ask; Is the love for a spouse the same as the love felt for a child? Is the love for a parent the same as for a more distant relative? Perhaps not! Is all LOVE that is felt always so warm, pure, positive and good? Not according to the decades of intense research performed on this topic.

Many have suffered from some form of loss of a companion, or separation, that has caused great distress in their lives. The many viewpoints contained within this book will attempt to address some of the distressing questions that you may have asked yourself recently or in the distant past. Questions such as; "What went wrong? What could I have done to prevent this from happening? Why has this happened to me? What will I do, and where do I go from here?". We will also address some of the questions we often fail to ask both to ourselves and to others. Let's explore further!

Chapter 1 - Cold Love

The subject of Cold Love will explore some of the numerous feelings that we have received, and perhaps given, within those relationships that destroy an innermost intimate part of ourselves. Cold Love is a love absence of sincerity, not pure or warm, and perhaps not even realized by most. Cold Love can be caused by loving someone for the wrong reasons or being loved for the wrong reasons. It is one's wrongful interpretation of sincere giving and receiving. It is emotions without true caring and innermost wisdom.

One may fool another, but you cannot fool yourself, or at least not for an extended period of time. You may think that you are in control of a particular situation, be it love or life, but how does it affect you when all of your logic falls apart?

Pure Love and Cold Love has existed throughout time, defining the entire spectrum of love, and in its extent. Yet most recently, it appears that Cold Love has evolved as a *dominant societal psychological attitude*, perhaps even acceptable by some. Not as a form of anti-love, but as facets of love. Perhaps not something that is given in anger, but more of an unintentional or subconscious reaction.

Throughout this journey, we will search for our personal truth. Truth from within ourselves, and of how we view others. We will explore our innermost perceptions of love, and perhaps our misunderstanding as well. How valid is our insight, how sound is our wisdom?

What makes any person an authority on "Cold Love"? You will not find its definition in Webster's, Wikipedia, or any other books that I am aware of, although many songs have been written which do reference its many traits. One becomes knowledgeable of such by experiencing and being aware of the encounters with Cold Love. Realization becomes a gift of knowledge and placed upon the persons experiencing the action and seeing the truth from several viewpoints. Not one-sided, not from a narrow perspective. Only by the experience, and by taking responsibility for your part in it, can one truly know the destructive forces of Cold Love, and then learn to take control of your interactions with it, to some degree.

No person is immune to Cold Love, and there are no known medications to prescribe as a cure. The destructive forces that Cold Love has presented in many lives may have forced them to examine their understanding of truth. It has forced a more-pure unclouded understanding of other's intentions, and self-reflection. By examining the effects of Cold Love with so many people over the past several decades, it has allowed many to see the harm presented to them and what effect it has had on their life as well.

Cold Love has presented a new awareness of what "Pure Love" should be, and allowed many others to understand the lack of it in today's societal interactions. The work contained within this book does not purely examine my personal understanding of Cold Love, it more so expresses the viewpoint of many-many others. Untold hours were spent researching and discussions with so many in order to gain a common interpretation of Cold Love, which I find extremely valid and very relevant to us all. While you read these words, try to envision what is being said, immerse yourself in a new understanding.

In preparation for the release of my writing, I had asked several of my associates to review and offer comments. One friend stated; You should present to your readers "a way out". What they are referring to is their interpretation of some of the information contained within this book. I agree, these words and analogies are not always heart-warming and sweet like apple pie, because they are meant to inform, not soft-shoe the issue. I listened to the feedback received and wondered as to how others would perceive this book and what could be said to comfort them. Several days later it hit me! Yes, I am presenting to my readers, "a way out" of the situations that are inherent with Cold Love. I am helping them to become aware.

Once we become aware, this is the beginning of our true adventure into a more-pure loving life. We become more conscious of life's loves, bitter and sweet. As our knowledge is enhanced, we become more in-tune with our true purpose. Once we understand this, "truth of ourselves", we then may understand that life will exist even if we suffer. So, let us diminish our suffering to some degree, at minimum.

Why do we place ourselves into relationships and situations that could be our undoing? Are we so desperate as we disavow the true ways of the world? Or, will we be so content as we deny our heart's true needs?

Knowing, understanding, feeling, sensing our awareness is the way to a more peaceful existence. Cold Love can never be struck down completely by mankind because Cold Love dominates our weaknesses and feeds on our fears and loneliness.

Now, let's continue our journey, and become aware.

Chapter 2 - Relationships

Let us examine our relationships with others, now and from the past. Would it help in your understanding? Could it make a difference if you were to learn that when the relationship failed it may not have been your fault? Or was it? Maybe you did all that you could or knew how to do, based on your current understanding of "what Love is". Perhaps your past relationship was doomed from the very start because your view-point of "what Love is" was skewed by your *interpersonal interpretation* of what Love is supposed to be, or what you have been taught, rather than what it was. Because of the situations that we put ourselves in, we may have set the stage for failure right from the beginning.

We all search for the love that we can hold deep in our hearts. That one true everlasting relationship. We enter into a relationship with hope, and honorable anticipation. Hoping that our wisdom will guide us through this at times foreboding enactment. Through every door that opens, we must choose a direction, and we do so with faithful anticipation.

Are we basing our decisions on truth, or what we hope to be true? Sometimes we try fooling ourselves into thinking that this is the one, our soulmate. Who among us does not want this journey for true love to end?

Have you not even once before convinced yourself that you could deal with a person's general attitude toward you, in justification for staying in a questionable situation, or for becoming involved in a relationship that felt forced? At the same time, we may be asking ourselves; "Is this truly the person that I want to spend my time with, and invest my love and trust in?". Maybe at some point in the relationship, we think that we could do better, but giving up on someone is like walking through a darkened path with no certainty of a brighter day.

We try to love, but within our hearts, we are not truly happy. Something is wrong! Something is missing! It is too hard; perhaps a hidden problem exists. The love that we are feeling should fill the void within because that is what pure love is supposed to do. But for some mysterious reason, that not-so-good sense echoes within our soul.

We must understand that companionship is a regal thing, but may become a hasty trap in some relationships. Time passes without a true self-examination of what we truly want out of life. Do we truly understand that by asking ourselves certain questions, and not having satisfying answers, or not answering honestly, we are putting ourselves on the road to disaster?

Why are we so uncertain of this situation that we have created? Why do we not give a true evaluation of where we stand, and stop kidding ourselves? Why do we hesitate when so much is at stake? Why do we so easily place our happiness in jeopardy when our entire relationship life is at risk?

What if we are responsible for all of the troubles and conflicts that have occurred? OK, perhaps not directly but indirectly? Have we set up our lives in such a way that we cannot resolve the conflicts? Is this conflict arising from outside influencing, or from within ourselves? If we allow ourselves to enter into situations that are not truly satisfying, then who more pays the price?

Why keep yourself in situations that are tearing you apart mentally? I am not only talking about a personal relationship as other types of relationships can be damaging as well. I am referring to your interpretations of your own life and beliefs.

If you are not happy, then stop reacting in the same old ways to what you have created, and stop placing yourself in the same types of situations. Take a good honest look at your life. Take a good look at yourself, and what you truly want to accomplish during your short time here on this earth.

Chapter 3 - Cold Love, A Facet of Love

We must understand that no one person holds the key to true love, as that key is as different as our individuality. Love is as different as the person in which it dwells. There are truly many facets to this spectrum we call Love. Every level of love's emotion that could be interrupted is contained within this spectrum. Each level containing its various counterparts. I am sure that each of us has felt different forms of love for each person that we have held dear.

As we explore the many facets of love, we may sense many things that we aren't quite sure of. We may question whether a certain situation could be considered or classified as real love. Perhaps you understood your true motivations for entering into a relationship or came to understand the other person's self-serving interest. The correlation that I want to point out here is that when we love for the wrong reasons, we are expressing Cold Love.

We have grown so comfortable with our modern-day acceptance of what love and hate looks or sounds like. When someone that we once loved turns on us, then we may feel hate toward them. Pretty cut and dried, isn't it? Perhaps not!

What could cause any person to hate another? Had love gone bad perhaps? An inexplicable swing from one end of the spectrum to the other? Maybe this too is an expression of Cold Love. Many have heard the adage, "you can hate someone to the same degree that you felt love for them". This may be true, but I think it is better expressed; "you can hate someone to the same degree that they felt Cold Love for them".

Cold Love is what True Love will never be. True Love is unconditional, never self-serving. True love is caring about someone for all of the right reasons. Even if the relationship is short-lived, you still feel love for that person thereafter. With Cold Love, if someone departs from the relationship, you feel hatred toward them, or perhaps they feel hatred toward you. Why can't we question as to where these emotions come from? When we hate, or we are hated, is it because of some emotional or physical need that can no longer be fulfilled by someone? We must come to an understanding of this destructive dependency and allow it to be washed away from our most inner self.

Understanding the spectrums of Cold Love will help us to see the unbalancing of emotions that we may not have conscious control of. Many people among us may not be aware of the hurt that they cause to others, yet still many know the harm they are causing and care little about who they hurt or use to get what they want.

If you are trying to pull your life together, you are on a personal quest to face the truth, that truth that only fits your inner reasoning. You want to understand your true wants, needs, and personal desires. Admitting that these are lacking from your life may strengthen your desire to obtain them.

Our quest must begin within ourselves. To truly understand the effects that Cold Love has played on our life, we must envision the many spectrums of hidden emotions lying beyond our *supraliminal discipline.*

Throughout time, mankind has searched their souls for the reason why we must love and need to be loved. Perhaps judging our existence on how much someone may or should love us. Have we not measured self-worth on these scales, or passed unfair judgment upon ourselves and others as we conclude?

Our past and present relationships likely contain many levels or spectrums of love, and at times we do not truly comprehend that which are most rewarding. Not by cognizant chose perhaps, but here we are nonetheless. Would it shock you to realize that our entire existence is built around spectrums?

Consider first our finely tuned spectrum of sound, or what we can hear. To humans, sounds are audible (capable of being heard), if the frequencies are between 20 and 20,000 vibrations per second. Is what we here all there is to be heard? Not by any measure! There exist far more beyond our finely tuned sense of hearing that could never be heard without special equipment or conversion.

Consider the entire electromagnetic spectrum ranging from Gamma Rays to Radio Waves. Humans have a very limited ability to see only the "Visible" portion of this entire spectrum, yet far more exist that we can't see with the naked eye. Our eyes are translating only a very small portion of the many spectrums of light (electromagnetic radiation) that exist. The human eye is only translating visible light wavelengths that range from 400 to 750 nanometers. Is what we see all there is to be seen? Even to mention the spectrums of life that is beyond our conscious awareness should swing open the gates to the eternal. Why should the spectrums of love be any less limitless or complicated?

Why is it that hate can dwell within us? Perhaps incomprehensible initially that we could hate someone to the same degree that we feel or felt love for them? Do we truly understand that by definition, love cannot be fully understood without hate? Without one, the other cannot be measured. This statement is not to imply that we cannot dislike someone's actions or traits without harboring some degree of love for them. It is an open statement that refers to the kind of hurt that we feel when someone that we have loved has turned away from us, creating an inner darkening of emotions which is an expression of Cold Love.

For each day that has passed, somewhere, someone has killed or maimed, all in the name of love. Wars have been fought taking numerous lives, destroying friends and families, all for the same. If you truly believe that love is so pure, how could these things happen? If this emotion is so one-sided then how could one hurt or take another's life, in the name of love? How strong has your love or rage elevated for someone? The more that you cared for that person, the more intensely they can hurt you, and the more intensely you may feel Cold Love for them. It is not to say that if you feel hatred for someone that you are a giver of Cold Love. It is more of how you express your hurt that falls into the spectrums of Cold Love.

Anyone that knows their inner self is surely aware that you cannot love two people in the same way, or at the same intensity. Everyone plays a different role in your spectrum of love. How many different forms of love have you known in your life? How many different emotions have you felt for the sum of them? It is most likely that each form of love felt has affected your life, and emotions, in such diversity that our minds are overwhelmed at times with memories of bittersweet.

Contained within the centuries of our existence, are acts of cruelty and barbarism directed toward the ones that we so-called "loved". Atrocities beyond the imaginations of the pure at heart have been inflicted on those that seek only true love and a kind heart to share their life.

Cold Love is as much a part of our culture as marriage. I am not implying that a direct connection exists, only that it is just as common. Some may relate sex to Cold Love, but in reality, it differs in several ways. One may make love to someone, or have sex with them. If the involved partners are honest with each other, then sincerity exists. Even in some purely sexual relationships, you can find sincerity. If one is deceiving another, then one could never make love to the other. If the act is purely sexual and self-serving, then the actions become a form of Cold Love.

Ask yourself, "how many times have you had sexual relations with your companion for no apparent reason, or just to exhaust yourself in preparation for a good night's sleep"? Was it an act purely for their satisfaction or perhaps your own? If you can remember the last time, then you need to consider the consequence. We must question motives within ourselves and others, to find the truth, and to understand the consequences.

Have we grown so willing, so content, to accept things only as they appear? Few of us have found that untainted form of happiness that flees our wonderment and haunts our skepticism. Are we truly content with what we have, or are we playing it safe?

What aspect or form of Cold Love is changing your life and obscuring your happiness? Denial cannot shelter this dark cloud of forbidden pleasure and pain. Cold Love is an addiction, as harmful as any drug when used abusively. We must allow truth and growth to lay our path ahead. Will we seek out and follow our true path? Few other avenues will deliver our souls to peace and happiness. Understand, and you will know. Knowledge is the gate key keeper.

Chapter 4 - Exploring Your Inner Self

Do you consider that you are in a good relationship? Can you still relate intimately to your spouse or companion? Do you feel loved, when you make love? Have you ever looked at your partner and said to yourself, "I can do better than this"? When was the last time that you held your so-called loved one with warmth, with no thoughts of another? Can you remember the last sensual kiss that passed your lips? Are you tasting the bitter fruit, or bearing it?

These are hard questions to ask and answer. Perhaps questions are residing deep within ourselves that if left unresolved will fester and cause long-term damage? At what point in our lives is it best to start dealing with these unresolved issues? If we had begun this exploration before now, how much better off could our life be now? We must attempt the break-down of these blinding barriers. Your accomplishment of this task will be measured as a great interpersonal achievement. Your level of achievement can be determined by how much wisdom you gained from your past experiences. Be honest with yourself, face the hard facts.

Do you feel that you are being loved for the right reasons? Have you considered the responses you receive from someone, and wondered just what did they mean by the little innuendoes that you detected? Have you posed the question to another, "what is it about me that you like or love"? Did you receive a positive and kind response, or, was the question sidestepped, or made light of?

The intent here is not to make ourselves feel guilty, or ashamed, but to uncover some hidden truths within ourselves. To explore some of the reasons why mankind has evolved into this *archetype of personalities* that we at times cannot tolerate, both from others and from within ourselves.

We must understand that throughout our lives we have been programmed to believe in certain things, or in a specified way. Are these beliefs skewed, biased, or even true for you? We are all the product of our innermost programming. Our unconscious minds will automatically react to outside stimuli based our what we have been programmed to do, or how to feel. We carry on throughout our lives with only that understanding that we have allowed ourselves to see. Our emotions are merely interpretations set forth by this innermost programming. If we have a desire to change our outlook on life, how we perceive, or how to find a different way of understanding, then we must start at the root of our understanding. We must understand that in which we are reacting to could be beyond our cognizant commands. Information that is chemically stored deep within our subconscious cause reactions to situations, and those reactions may not be proper.

Sigmund Freud was one of the greatest phycological minds of the 19th and 20th centuries, and theorized that our "unconscious mind" plays a vital role in overall behavior, and that our thoughts and feelings operate below the threshold of ordinary awareness. Freud is often viewed as the grandfather of phycological study, one that revolutionized how modern-day cultures think about human psyche. Freud defined specific facets of our personalities, familiar to many as the "id" and the "superego". The "id" is related to our biological, simplistically referred to as our inherent nature, or basic desires of hunger, thirst, desire, and aggression. The "superego" is the internalization of all the rules, values, and expectations that we absorb when living in a certain culture, society, and that which is very influential like a particular family environment. Freud also believed that our unconscious mind has great influence in what we dream.

Let us compare this situation to the programming of a computer. Let us say that a computer has been programmed to answer a particular query with a specified result. The data inputted, results in a return of information in the form of an answer. Is the answer returned correct, or is it merely an answer? Keep in mind that a computer can be programmed to return the sum of 2+2 to equal 7. Our innermost programming, or subconscious, or psyche, can as well usher us into a total misunderstanding of situations in our everyday life. Could our programming be flawed? If so, can we, or how can we correct it?

Let us explore the inner truth, and allow our life a new meaning. A new way if you will, to see life, ourselves, and our relationships. A truer understanding of our actions, their imposing consequence on us and others, and how they character our innermost self. Let us open our minds, and renew our beliefs.

We cannot continue blaming ourselves or others for what we had hoped would happen. Using every excuse imaginable, and allowing this way of life to continue. We have paved this path we chose to walk. We are to blame for any hidden shame. If we don't take action to correct our life, will we continue to live in regret? Time is passing quickly with a limited about of days remaining. We should be living life, not just existing through it. Let us somehow make things right, or at minimum a bit better. We should care enough about ourselves to at least give it a good try?

Throughout this text, you may notice that the word, "ourselves" used very frequently. One of the reasons for this exploration is so we can take a look at the "self" that we express every day. That person we can't hide from or deceive. Remember that we are never too young, too old, too poor, or too rich, to be unhappy.

Where you come from is not as important as how far your life has progressed from its starting point. Are you a better person now than a year before? Have you gained insight or wisdom that presents positives in your life? Has your heart filled with love or dismay? We enter cross-roads throughout our lives and each choice we make was an opportunity and our choice to make. If we have strayed from our chosen path then who is to say that we cannot return. How could anyone find their true soul without knowing, "self". We must understand that the past cannot be changed, but the way we live the remainder of our life is still in our control.

Some feel that if they can control others, then they have conquered fate. They truly feel that they are in control. The reality is that, we, as physical beings, are never totally in control. We must ask ourselves, "what do we hope to accomplish by even trying to control others"? Any attempt to control others is self-destructive. You may, without realizing, destroy their spirit, and your own. Anyone that considers that they can control another's beliefs is often found to be a fool and may find themselves alone in their journey.

When one person exerts so much control over another, one opinion is obliterated, a different and unique view is lost to the depths of adversity. We all must understand that the only real option is to control our understanding, what makes us tick. Do we truly understand how words or deeds affect us, or others as a complete person?

We must strip ourselves down emotionally, beyond what we have been led to believe about ourselves, and others. We must open our minds and allow a new understanding as if to re-live our lives, or at least a portion of it, through different eyes or view-points.

Has someone in your life told you that you are not attractive, or that you are not good enough for them? Said only a few times, we may write it off as someone just letting off steam, or maybe they are just being cruel. But said enough, it can influence your innermost programming, and affect how you relate to yourself, disintegrating your measure of self-worth.

You know that you are a good person, but someone has seen fit to cut you down to a lower level, or bring you down to their level. A level that you are not comfortable with. Your understanding of life and love is now jaded. What is the purpose? Maybe it was to allow them some sort of control over you, something that they must accomplish. But inside your heart, you cannot see a meaningful or positive purpose. You only feel the hurt, the doubt, the misfortune. You try to speak to this person in hopes of obtaining some sort of understanding of why they are treating you this way. Almost everyone knows that most situations or conflicts could be resolved through communication, but few exercise this *innate knowledge*.

Let us say that you are fortunate enough to convince your mate that talking about what is disturbing you could resolve the issue. You sit calmly with them and begin to touch on subjects that need to be discussed. If you can get through the next few moments talking calmly with kindness and sincere interaction, you may have a chance of making some form of resolution that would allow growth. However, if you are dealing with someone that is interpreting the relationship under the influence of Cold Love, you may ignite a fuse that leads to an assortment of uncontrolled emotions. They may at first be cooperative, yet soon you notice a lack of calm in their manner. Most of their time is being spent thinking about what they are going to say in rebuttal, rather than truly listening to your concerns. Do you find that you are frequently being interrupted? Is it hard for you to even finish your train of thought? It's not always easy to be open and honest, which is the root of most problems.

Just by bringing up certain topics, you are declaring that you are seeing through their game playing. You are placing them on the defensive end of the conversation, and things may soon get out of hand as they attempt a guarding of themselves. They will give lengthy explanations to your questions, banter that doesn't often make sense. Then, if they fail to sway you with their mental manipulation, they become irritated, you know, they start throwing the past in your face, that sort of thing. Most of us have been there, no one could enjoy it. At this point, you may begin trying to extract yourself from the conversation without igniting their more violent emotions or actions, with no progress gained.

If this person were to allow you to see his or her true intentions, they would be giving up the physiological ground they feel that they hold over you. Perhaps they feel that you would leave them if you knew them well enough. They feel that they must keep you down for you to see them as somewhat superior. If they can keep you down, then they feel less threatened that you may leave and find someone else, perhaps better suited for you. They require that physiological off-balancing of your inner beliefs to keep you thinking about what you did wrong, instead of what you believe to be right. It was once stated that; "because you choose to look down on everyone else, doesn't mean that they will look up to you", which I find to be profoundly true.

How do you feel about yourself, truly? When someone, perhaps a stranger, pays you a sensual compliment, how do you react? Do you accept the praise, or does it upset you because this is something that you expect to get from your loved one? You may question the validity of the praise, concluding that they want something more than you are prepared to give. If you are not getting complimentary praise from that special someone in your life, then you may consider that someone else just may not know you as well, and the compliment is unworthy. Perhaps these are indicators that Cold Love has already taken on a strong influence in your understanding of your self-worth.

Is this truly the way that you want to live out your life? Never knowing your true potential? Never allowing yourself to have the kind of friends that you can care deeply for, unselfishly? Being made to think that you already have the best, or more than you deserve? Living in a mental imbalance to the point that you don't even know your true self? It is as if the person that you once were has died off. Once you realized your current position, this can be changed. Just being aware is a great starting point.

If you can question what is going on in your life, and seek out a greater meaning, you are placing yourself on the road to a brighter future. With a better understanding of yourself and others you are better prepared to make more sound decisions in directing your life. Once the right paths are taken you will soon see that happiness can and will find you.

If you can find some quiet time to think, and if by what you are now reading is causing you to question your understanding, then you are on the right path. Your personnel path. Believe in yourself. You can be the best friend that you have ever known, both to yourself and others. No one else could know your true intentions. No one else can correct your understanding and see the true person you are, no one more than you.

If you have become a victim of Cold Love, let's find a way to shield your life from it. We must understand what has occurred or what is occurring to hurt you, and make the necessary changes. We all need to understand that as a victim of Cold Love, we may be unintentionally passing on our life's interpretations onto others, and we may be involuntarily victimizing them. They too deserve better, the same as you.

Chapter 5 - We the Victims

Street crime, abusive drug use, homelessness, abandonment, hustlers, infidelity, fraud. These are a mere fraction of the components that plague our world. It is hard to imagine that with so many harmful elements infesting our society that anyone could escape being a victim. Many have sought a remedy that would rid our worldly existence of such hurts and hatred, but few understand that we are likely propagating these traits from generation to generation merely by allowing them to dominate our psyche. Not by choice or conscious actions perhaps, but nevertheless, we are. Who will stop the cycle if not us?

What comes to mind when you say the words, "We the victims"? Take a moment and contemplate. Try to see the self-portrait that you paint yourself. Do you consider yourself to be a victim? If so, then further ask of yourself; "are you a victim by means of other's actions, or of your self-inflicted errors?" We have to overcome the distressful intentions that are presented to us in everyday life. We have little control over others, but we can prevent their interactions into our understanding of what is right, and what is wrong.

We must never consider that if we are hurt by others then it is proper to hurt in return. Turn-about is not always fair play. If this is your understanding, then you are promoting the hurt filled acts. You have gone beyond being a victim, you have become an offender. When you now become the culprit, passing on the pain, then you become a victim of not only others but of yourself. How can you convince yourself, that you can do unto others what has caused you pain? This creates severe guilt within your inner-self because you have personal knowledge of how much these actions can hurt. In these modern times of dog-eat-dog, we have to consider where our distress is coming from, find ways to shield ourselves from it, and never pass it on to others.

Knowing the origin of our distress is essential in the healing process and the prevention of future problems. Taking responsibility for your understanding of how life, and love works is an essential key in developing a better way of doing things. We can change and adapt, it's up to us. We may not be able to change other's interpretations and understanding, but we can prevent a great deal the self-inflicted crisis that seems to plague our lives.

Learning from your mistakes may not always be enough. A mistake made during a particular situation was unique to that situation, and that unique situation may never be repeated to an exact degree. So, you may ask; "what good has the experience served"? Through your experiences, you should acquire knowledge, and this form of wisdom most often equates to more than its face value. Wisdom is not merely a fragment of learning, it also allows us to mold our attitude toward our inner self, and should be reflected in our actions toward others. Having the wisdom of a situation is not enough, it must be exercised and expressed. One situation may not appear to be the exact same as another, although fragments of the situations may be common. Use what you have learned from previous mistakes, even if only fragments are similar, and try for that more positive result.

Have you ever hurt so intensely that you could not believe that life could be so cruel? Your stomach tied in knots, your heart racing to the point that you thought it would explode, felt that lump in your throat preventing you from swallowing easily. Who would have thought that emotional suffering could cause such a physical manifestation? Who could judge physical pain to be more extreme or intense than mental anguish?

As defined, a victim may be someone that is sacrificed or injured under any of various conditions. For example; if you gave so much of yourself to a relationship, only to be abandoned, this may place you in the category of being a victim of that situation. In that situation, the other party may be considered the culprit.

Now, for a new consideration. What about the times you may have sacrificed your true emotions and placed yourself in a not-so-good situation yet at the time you thought was good for you? What harm did you create for yourself? Was the sacrifice made worth the price that you must now pay? Thereby, is it not true that a person can create a situation in which they become both the culprit and the victim?
If you find yourself thinking that only wrong was done to you, please remember, "you made sacrifices when you entered into the relationship". Who did you hurt the most? For all of the You that you gave up, for all of the relinquished dreams, there has to be a price to pay. If we conform to what we truly believe about ourselves and try to do what we know is right or best for all concerned, then our chances of finding true love in our lives are greatly increased.

OK, back to relationships. You were involved in some form of a relationship, and you were deceived. Into this deception, you must understand that the other party involved either was unclear of their emotions and true feeling toward you or perhaps they have a cold heart that is incapable of true and honest expression. It may not be of considerable consolation to you, but think of what this person has deprived themselves of. Many in this world can never know true love, especially those living within the boundaries of Cold Love. Their narrow insight prevents them from realizing the greatest emotion known to man. Share this book with them. Share what you now know about yourself.

The age-old question, "WHY?". Do you feel that there were times in your life when you were being sacrificed? The lingering question may have been, "WHY is this happening to me". For us to reap all that this situation has to offer, we should be asking ourselves, "why did I allow this situation into my life?" Not necessarily to place blame on yourself, just to re-evaluate the situation. After all, the purpose of this book-adventure effort is to better understand the view-points other than that of which our understanding has concluded previously, right!

Let us say that a particular situation in your life qualifies you as a victim. What are the elements that contributes to this conclusion? Could one's understanding of life be programmed to react to certain stimuli in a particular manner that may have caused bad judgment, or was it just an unfortunate situation?

Consider this: For many years of your existence from earliest of childhood, through adolescence, well into adulthood, someone has been telling you what to believe, what was true about a particular situation, and how you should react to it. How could we not allow others to influence our understanding of life? As a child, we need interpretation to assist in our conclusions. Young minds are always eager to listen, absorbing information like a sponge. But, how do you teach a child that your interpretation is a singular view-point, an opinion? Most parents do not consider this form of analogy when molding a young mind, then they question why a child becomes rebellious or turns out to be like them as adults, further propagating the issue.

We must understand that we are often taught on a singular plane of comprehension. Situations throughout our life will occur which are unlike our understanding of what may have happened in the past, we must recognize the differences and adapt. It is the nature of things, and of life itself, that change is constant. If a parent is forceful in their version of right and/or wrong, they may stifle a child's instincts. Any constructive reasoning skills that would have been inherent to their nature may have been met with undue criticism, thus causing them to shelter or disconnect from a special ability. A child's total environment is a looking glass into the world that they are hoping to understand. Every second of their life is molding their future. We are a product of our past *environmental hereditation* and our *genetically inherent traits* that survive the ordeal. No one ever said that growing up and being a responsible adult was easy, so why make the process harder for them than it has to be.

You may consider that an inherent trait was created in your past, therefore it cannot be changed. Please understand that our quest is not an attempt to re-create the past, but to come to a clearer understanding of how our past molds our current perceptions, and how we can insightfully control our reactions to stimuli and viewpoints in order to enhance our future state of mind.

Being a victim does not always entitle us to special consideration from others. Most often the victims are left with little or no compensation for their losses. There are at least two options presented to a victim. They can either brand themselves with the mark of self-pity, or, learn from the negative experience and move on to a better tomorrow.

The mark of self-pity is not only self-defeating, but it also expresses your vulnerability to others. When we learn from our negative experiences, we extract a pearl of positive wisdom from the situation and our retrospect is enhanced to a point that aids in shielding our lives from similar occurrences.

In most relationships, Cold Love is expressed in all the ways that make us unhappy. During the many arguments that occur, we often sense and express versions, or levels, of Cold Love. Have you ever come to the point in a discussion when you considered that you or your partner were merely bantering? This form of communication is quite familiar to most of us. At first, it may appear witty or as playful teasing. But later as the conversation reels throughout your memory, other interpretation arises. Is it possible that this bantering is masking true feelings or cryptically expressing doubt and distrust? Now that you have replayed the words and content, you discover a *satirical wit* that was totally out of place in your exchange of views.

Although mentally reliving an argument or conversation may be painful, it allows our interpretation an opportunity to more clearly define our understanding of the situation. Once understood, your direction can be self-defined without someone constantly directing your thoughts, and misleading your conclusions. There is hope for all that find themselves in bad situations. The first step is to stop the interactions that make you a victim and then by not propagating the hurt filled actions.

Chapter 6 - Fueling the Fire

Cold Love can become a disintegrating effect on a person's life if allowed, and often without us even being aware of it. Many underlying variables exist that can spark-off this hidden obscure form of emotional state, and many of us will react to it harshly or defensively. Cold Love is not the problem in and of itself, it is our negative reaction to the issues presented or how we handle the event. A correlation can be seen between the reactions to Cold Love's effects and a glitch in a software program. Consider the many times you use your computer for months and things go along just fine for that time, then all of a sudden, the software starts to show glitches or problems in its execution for no apparent reason. Let's face it, our perceptions change over time due to numerous new issues encountered which either enhance or flaw what we once believed to be true.

Within our *mental programming*, depending on the severity, these glitches can be so deep-seated into our understanding that we may only see the wrong that others commit against us, not realizing that our obscure version of the situation is now tainted. For example; being *self-righteous* can be devastating to our everyday lives as we interact with others. We can't be right about everything, nor can our version of right be projected onto others.

Our minds can often react without truly understanding the whole truth. Whole truth being; what is analogous from two or more perspectives. Studies have shown that our reactions to outside stimuli are most often guided by our level of *emotional intelligence*. Without exploring and seeking to develop our emotional reactions to outside stimuli, our mental programming can become flawed, just as a computer program can develop glitches or bugs over time, as discussed above. We must understand that those things that we feel so certain of is primarily true only within our understanding and that moment's perception. Plus, our inner truth may only be accepted within a fixed set of circumstances, yet not all happenstances.

Some may often feel as if they do not fit into what is considered normal. Then, the all-important question arises, "what is normal?". We live our lives in what we consider as reality, but when that realism is challenged, we feel set apart from what seems to be the reality that others live in. In truth, others may be feeling the same distress, or doubt that they may not be on the right road to happiness. All *corporeal beings* are vulnerable, it is just that some have a higher degree of emotional intelligence that allows them to deal with specific forms of stimuli in a more calm and *cognizant* manner.

Our harsh judgment of others can become one of the primary triggers which allow Cold Love to become a factor in our understanding. Our judgment of others, or a particular situation, is not merely an interpretation of facts, it is a momentary judgment of what we believe to be true, or what is referred to as a "*snap-judgment*". This form of judgment may not reflect a true explanation of the moment's reality. These hasty judgments may also contain *interpolations*, or an introduction of erroneous information extrapolated from our narrow perception of who or what we believe someone could be. At that moment you may believe it to be true, but in reality, isn't it a biased truth at best. There are exceptions however. Those times when our exacting judgment was spot-on, but this is not often found to be the norm.

When trying to understand the actions of others, our minds will frequently use extrapolation to fill in the unknowns, and what we inject may be far worse than the reality of the situation. At this time, try to remember that Cold Love is often lurking in the background to seize the moment, to inject negatives that allow you to conclude a very undesirable outcome. If a mutual trust was lacking in the relationship and if your devotion and love was stronger than your mates, then we have to ask ourselves, "did we fuel the fire of Cold Love", by allowing this to happen?

Recall a time when you waited for someone to arrive on-time. Perhaps to pick you up for a date, or maybe to come home to you at the end of the day. At that point when they are considered to be very late, and they haven't called or messaged you for hours, your mind has no idea where they are or who they are with. You may feel as if your world, or at least your reality, is coming to an end. Perhaps this is not the first time this has happened, but all times previous you rationalized the situation to allow yourself to believe what your heart wanted to believe. You convince yourself that this is easier than facing the truth.

Within the timeframe of the failed relationship, even at the very beginning, did it feel entirely right for you, a whole-hearted connection on all levels? Maybe you connected on a few levels, so you considered that to be enough, or at least enough at that time. As we often do, you may have felt that the overall connection would grow over time, as you become more familiar with each other. However, as time passed, the sexual connection started to diminish. Those times of holding each other close became less frequent, even the passionate kisses seemed to have died-off. Did there come a time when you were around other people and your mate's attention started to wane as they seemed to be focused more on others than on you, not like before when your relationship was still young? If we can't understand how we allowed Cold Love into our life, then we are doomed to fueling that fire over and over again until it consumes who we once were.

Some may be so privileged to live out their entire life not knowing the damage that Cold Love brings, but for many others, it is present early on, even in childhood. What allows anyone to think that their parents were not exchanging forms of Cold Love, and if so, then they may have been raised thinking that the parents' interactions with each other were normal and acceptable. This is the process of *propagation* or passing certain traits or beliefs onto the next generation.

There exist numerous studies relating to specific types of traits and how they affect our lives. A once-prominent Phycologist by the name of Gordon Allport performed years of studies relating to how specific traits in our personality play out in our interactions with others, and to some degree creates our mental environment. If we allow Cold Love to become part of our personality or affect our traits, then according to Allport, these can work together to form our overall personality. Thereby, we must learn not only what affects Cold Love is presenting in our lives but we need to learn how to diminish those effects. Allport also eludes to the fact that negative traits will hold us back, hampering our mental growth, tainting our view of ourselves and the role we play throughout our life.

Chapter 7 - Cold Love vs Emotional Intelligence

Many of us may have studied what is referred to as *"Emotional Intelligence"*, or "E.I.", as opposed to the more popular "Intelligent Quotient", or "I.Q." which is quite different. I.Q. is more a measure of how well a person can reason with known facts and process that information to draw a viable conclusion. I.Q. is quantifiable using multiple testing methods to determine a person's mental age score, then applying that score to the following formula; Mental age score / chronological age x 100 = I.Q. Score.

Many books have been written on the subject of Emotional Intelligence, yet as of today there exist no formal psychometric test or scale to present a reliable finding. The reasoning is that E.I. is dependent upon the emotional state of a person at a specific time and the situational stimuli encountered. Being that each can vary depending on everything from time-of-day, weather, cultural upbringing, religious factors, age, I.Q., educational level, personal health, even one's economic status. With so many fluctuating metrics to account for, a consensus or sound determination may not be possible.

Cold Love exist in abundance within people having a low level of Emotional Intelligence. Perhaps one could conclude that as the levels of E.I. are decreased, the effects of Cold Love on your life would increase. An emotionally intelligent individual is highly tuned to their own emotions, seldom acting in a self-serving manner. While a person allowing Cold Love to dominate their understandings will present negativity, often expressing their inner frustration, thus causing an emotional unsettling of everyone's emotional state. Interacting with others is a platform for Cold Love to present itself and not always in a subtle manner. It is not likely that a person with a higher level of E.I. would want to tolerate someone expressing Cold Love.

There is hope however. It is fortunate for mankind, that the skills necessary to increase one's level of Emotional Intelligence and to decrease the level of distress that Cold Love presents in everyday life, can be practiced and enhanced. Your ability to become a better romantic partner, leader, parent, or best friend is just before you. All you need to do is to become aware of the shortcomings and start working toward your goals. Raise your E.I. levels and you will soon find the negatives being replaced with positive results. Not an overnight fix, but a worthwhile goal nonetheless.

If Cold Love is dominate within a person's personality, they may never find the emotional safety that creates the required foundations for a person to feel safe. For an intimate relationship to blossom and become long-lasting, both parties have to feel safe with each other. How could a love mature if each person can't find that mature love that they seek? Feeling emotionally safe is important in any form of relationship.

Even if you had a good relationship initially, injecting any form of Cold Love will disintegrate that which was built, to a point when most feel that there is no way to fix the issue or understand what went wrong. The damage is done, unreconcilable! If your relationship becomes toxic or your partner appears clueless or unwilling, where do you look for help? What changed? Why did it change? The evaluation of the levels of emotional intelligence is a good start. You must first understand both your motivations and your partners intentions. If the relationship is worth saving, to both parties, then you have to get back to the basics of why you were together in the first place. If it is determined that one or both persons were simply fulfilling a short-term desire or need, then the relationship was doomed from the beginning.

Chapter 8 - Sense & Emotion

I had previously discussed that "hearing" was one of the prominent senses used when determining the judgments that we place on others, good, bad, or indifferent. If you dare to claim you are not one of those persons, then you are claiming that you have never met someone with a sexy, kind, soft, stern, or annoying voice, just to throw out some quick examples.

Our sense of "hearing", goes beyond what is commonly known as audible. Our understanding or judgment is not solely influenced by the words that we hear, but also how we interpret or perceive the information. The tone of the spoken word can nullify the intended root-facts of the statement. Want proof? In a harsh tone tell your mate, "I love you!". Then ask them if it sounded sincere. The point being, that when someone is distressed their verbal tones may be totally out of sync with their true intention. If Cold Love has a grip on their life, it may be extremely hard for this person to express their true feelings peacefully, or in a tone of sincerity.

Another factor that we must explore is "guilt". If I had to make a summarized statement about it, I would say; "guilt can ignite and fuel the fires of Cold Love". Guilt can rob us of our inner calm. Guilt has trespassed into our place of inner peace, that place we once knew as solitude. Once we become guilt-ridden, it's like a dark unwanted stranger that exists within our psyche which we must encounter and somehow deal with. What we must realize is, guilt can be a good emotion. Guilt, is our mind's way of expressing self-reproach for our wrongdoing, not only to others but to ourselves as well. Why can't we look at guilt as a guiding emotion? Guilt can be a valuable teacher if we take responsibility for our actions and accept *culpability*.

Anyone with a caring heart can feel the burden of guilt. We are not a perfected species, and at some point, in our lives we may transgress onto others. Even if our intentions were honorable, we can at times bring about hurt to someone, causing guilt.

Why can't we resolve the guilt? Guilt is merely an emotion caused by us wanting to be responsible, otherwise, we wouldn't care who we hurt, which many are capable of. Why must we indulge ourselves in its remorseful awareness? We must understand that once we become aware of having done something wrong, our reaction to that situation is what makes it right or wrong in the long-term.

If we have hurt someone, and then take action to make things right again and to prevent the situation from occurring again, then we become wiser and a better person for it. If at all possible, we not only resolve the issue, we become closer to that person. It is when we cause harm and try to counter our culpability by blaming others that guilt takes on a darker side. If guilt cannot act as an *admonishment* to our inner self then its purpose is forfeited, and its consequences can be perpetual.

What about those people who often make you feel guilty, even for seemingly inconsequential things? Why would anyone want to cause another to feel guilty, you may ask? Perhaps because "guilt" is an instrument to the contributors of Cold Love. They see "passing guilt" as a way to enhance their abilities to control others. Presenting undeserving guilt onto others acts as a cloak to conceal the misgivings that they refuse to take responsibility for. It's their short-term solution to preventing the facts from being discussed or to be known. It is their apprehension of facing their true inner self and a very uncertain future, a desperate attempt to control their inner thoughts and of others.

Is the giver of Cold Love always aware of what harm they are causing? Likely so, yet there may be exceptions. The hard fact is, not everyone will allow themselves to see their true self or the truth about who is more wrong. It's just easier for them to exist in their narrow self-righteous perspective of all things. Manipulating others has become a way of dealing with everyday life for them. A deep-seated thought process used either to set up an occurrence, mask intent, or to prevent something. Givers of Cold Love were taught, and learned perhaps unwillingly, that guilt is merely an instrument. A device used by another to accomplish a purpose.

There are other aspects of "guilt" that should be touched on. Think of a situation in your life when you felt guilty about something you did or didn't do. Why is it that you felt as if you had to pay a penalty for the offense? Depending on the severity of the offense, you may have *indemnified* the situation just by your realization, and admitting your culpability.

We all know in our hearts how to treat someone that we care about. Our conduct, especially in close relationships, is measured every moment that we interact or are involved with that person. Most of the time we are aware of when we are being kind, honest, and loving. In turn, we should also be aware of when we are being harsh, deceitful, and/or hateful. To infringe upon our own beliefs with that which we know to be wrong is a futile effort to convince ourselves that we have grounds to do so. In one single exertion, we have disarmed our integrity and corrupted our innocence.

What are these emotions that are invoked deep within us when we are being harsh, deceitful, or hateful? These expressions were presented to perhaps lash out at someone else, so why are we feeling so distressful? Recall that guilt is defined as a feeling of culpability for offenses, right. At the time, you may have felt within your right to lash-out at someone for their transgression against your love and trust, but at that same time, your actions may have caused a *paroxysm* of inner guilt. Even if the other person was totally at fault, you have unwillingly condemned yourself to feel guilty. If you are the one that has committed the transgression, then it should be clear to you why you are feeling guilty. Sometimes we try to turn the situation onto the other partner, making them feel as if our distress is being caused by their actions toward us. But we cannot hide from our inner truth. As easy as it seems to blame others, we still sense culpability. What offenses have you created that you can wash from your memory so easily?

Guilt is like a *malevolent* growth on your spiritual being. Seldom lying dormant, it is a vigilant infestation devouring all that is good inside you. Our only hope of exerting any authority over guilt is to flood our inner peace with love and hope for a brighter future. Once we accept responsibility for the hurt created in our life, we create a new path in which to build a new life and enhance our understanding.

Chapter 9 - Circumstantial Insight

Cold Love is further propagated by our misunderstanding of the many situations that surround us every day. Cold Love is like an atom of a molecule attaching itself to other molecules to form unwanted substances or circumstances. I would like to think that we can, in a sense, create circumstances in our lives that will dilute the effects of Cold Love, or at least help us to shield against it to some degree. By learning from our mistakes, we may relinquish, or at least dampen, some of the torment and inner-pain we feel. Taking a closer look at any unwanted circumstance we find ourselves entangled, we must first determine if it was self-inflicted or imposed upon us against our will.

No one wanting a clear conscious would abuse another intentionally, mentally or physically. But in many ways, we abuse ourselves without even realizing it. Many forms of deception can be defined as abusive. Cold Love not only deceives others, but it also betrays the host as well. Cold Love is abusive to mankind in general, with no known antidote. If there is any hope to contain or control to some degree Cold Love's destructive forces, we must begin with the single self. The "I" that is you.

How knowledgeable are you to the prejudicial conflicts that are eroding our global society? What injurious or damaging results are being presented by our judgments or actions placed on another, in total disregard of their feelings and human rights? What preconceived judgment or opinions do you contribute? Prejudice is abundant in this world filled with adverse learning, flourishing without just grounds or sufficient knowledge of our true purpose. What irrational attitudes or hostilities have we directed against an individual, a group, a race, or their imaginary characteristics? For each person having an opinion and belief, their conclusions are *extrapolations* formed by their mental storeroom of what they have been taught, what they have concluded within their own minds, what they believe to be true, and their personal knowledge of existence, even if that knowledge is flawed.

Some may question as to how any portion of their knowledge could be flawed, so let us present this simple example; At one point in your early life, you were taught that the color of grass is green. This belief appears straight forward and simple, until you learned later that the numerous compounds within the grass itself is merely reflecting the colors blue and yellow, absorbing all other visible light wavelengths, thereby you see what is interpreted by your visual receptors as the color green. This same form of analogies must be brought into our understanding of what we believe to be true in all aspects of life, our understanding of all things. This is not to suggest that we are wrong about everything that we believe to be true. Yet we must understand that Cold Love is a cloaked deceiver, powered by adverse thoughts and emotions, and it thrives on our misconceptions.

Another example to ponder; Look down at your hand. What do you see? Your mind quickly concludes that you see skin wrapped around some fingers and a thumb, right! Look deeper! What you are really seeing is a collection of molecules held together by a nuclear force that is vibrating at a specific atomic signature reflecting electromagnetic energy to your finite spectrum of vision. If you broke down these molecules into their various atoms, then peering into the atomic structure, you would see nothing, and the energy that exist could only be measured. As corporeal beings, we see and feel on a material plane of existence, but in reality, we are just a congealed grouping of energy. Energy that has transformed or evolved into substances. So, once again, look at your hand and behold. I am not trying to offer up a discussion on particle physics here, only an attempt to open one's mind to a deeper understanding of our existence and to understand that things are not always as they appear to be at first, and this holds true within our relationships as well.

Situations, as humans experience, are created by the interaction of space, time, and matter. Time is expressed by simple matter moving in or displacing space, and matter can be defined as *temporal*. There is so much that we as humans cannot, or as of yet, have not been allowed to see or understand. For any situation to occur in your life, there has to be another side to react or interact with. Try to see and understand that other view. Your life will be enriched with boundless possibilities, and a greater you will emerge.

Chapter 10 - Tolerance of Abuse or Exploitation

Over the years, throughout the numerous case studies accomplished, there existed a shared trait within many that most were very reluctant to discuss openly. The topic; Tolerance of Abuse or Exploitation. Here we discuss some the innermost personal thoughts from people that have allowed this form of Cold Love into their lives, at times knowingly, and were fortunate enough to have survived the ordeal. In some cases, a few subjects would disclose how, and why, they presented this misapplication of caring with total indifference. These are not easy topics for anyone to discuss with total honesty, but very necessary if we want to get back to a better way of living our life and heal the wounds.

Throughout this process, remind yourself that we are alone here reading these words and we don't have others listening to our thoughts or judging us. We have this opportunity to question ourselves and determine what went wrong and when.

Before we go further, let's take a quick look at a few forms of abuse and exploitation to see if they sound familiar to your situation;

- Psychological or Emotional Abuse; A form of abuse considered by a person exposing another person to behavior that may result in emotional disturbances, including anxiety, depression, and stress disorders. This form of abuse can occur when the balance of power is greatly skewed to a single person within the relationships and may evolve to display physical qualities if not resolved in the early stages.
- Domestic or Physical Abuse; Defined as chronic mistreatment in marriage, families, dating and other intimate relationships. Can include emotionally

abusive behavior although psychological abuse does not always lead to physical abuse, yet physical abuse in domestic relationships is nearly always preceded and accompanied by psychological abuse, as psychological aggression is the most reliable predictor of later physical aggression.

It may, or may not, be comforting to know that recent studies have found that heterosexual men and women physically and emotionally abuse each other at equal rates. A less recent and separate 14-year study reported that lesbian relationships have a higher overall rate of psychological aggression and emotional abuse than heterosexual or gay male relationships. Furthermore, women who have been involved with both men and women reported higher rates of abuse from their female partners.

It was also determined, unfortunate to all, that psychological aggression is so prevalent in dating relationships that it can be regarded as a normalized element of dating. Perhaps understanding the influences that Cold Love presents can assist in our understanding of these recent findings, yet disheartening all the same. There is so much about our nature that must be examined, the cause and effect, and the hard questions need to be addressed.

How many of us at times have allowed certain qualities of one person to out-weigh their negative impact on our life beyond what we can truly tolerate? Be it based on physical appearance, social attitude, scholastic aptitude, base theology, intellect or even sexual prowess, to some degree we have all likely formed some sort of predisposition toward others, even if it is buried deep within our subconscious. If any hope exists in better controlling these inner *predilections*, honestly confronting them is our best hope.

In our quest to find love and companionship, we will often make compromises to our Wishlist. Perhaps a person is not as physically attractive as we had desired, but you can feel that their heart has good intentions and they treat you with respect, so you take that chance of *appeasement.* Perhaps they are beautiful in their physical appearance, so you tolerate their ever-present not so pleasant attitude toward you. Is it our fear of being alone that is motivating, or skewing, our judgment? If we wish to find that which will make us whole, these are topics we must discuss.

Within my many years of research, I have found that if someone is made to feel secure, and they are treated with respect, the outward or physical appearance of their mate often played no significant role of importance. On the other hand, there are a lot of couples that stay in an abusive relationship just because their partner is very attractive physically or monetarily stable. We all make tradeoffs in one form or another. But are these trade-offs a form of selling-out, selling ourselves short, and how are they damaging our self-worth?

Who among us has not taken all of this into consideration at one point or another, even if we did not discuss the topic openly? We see among us everyday couples that just do not seem to belong together, a miss-fit of sorts. You may ask yourself, "what is their secret"? What does she see in him, or what does he see in her? I have asked those questions, not just to myself, but to many others as well. It may not be such a surprise to you, but the overall number one answer was "security".

Within our sense of security, we often find a form of atonement. We feel safe, at least for the time being. We rationalize that things are better than they were previously, so we must be doing something right. Something familiar that agrees with our understanding of how we want things to be. We find comfort in knowing what tomorrow will bring, even if it is only knowing who we will wake up with the next morning. If mutual security is the glue that binds your relationship over a long period, you may even consider yourself blessed. At least you have something perceptible and grounded to base your relationship on.

For many of us, uncertainty is the feeling most prominent. A strong sense of doubt that not only causes us to question our state of mind, it obscures our ability to make a sound judgment about ourselves and others. It causes hesitation in the acceptance of what could be the truth about our interactions. Are we one of those people who just can't handle the truth? We have all heard the phrase; Truth hurts!

If you are one of the lucky few that have been fortunate enough to have found someone that wants to care deeply for you, is honest and open with their intentions, then you should be very hesitant in your willingness to explore what else is out there. Think before you leap! Perfection can be found within an *atoned* perception.

How many times do we need to hear; the grass is not always greener on the other side? These words have validity, yet many continue to ignore them. Don't confuse your self-doubt with the uncertainties that you may sense in others, or other relationships, or allow your *wanderlust* to guide you. Only you can determine your future, and with each decision you make a consequence will occur, and if that decision is self-serving then there is a heavy price that must be paid.

Perhaps we all have a little shallowness within us, or should we say, being overly selective. Let us consider how the physical appearance of one's mate, reflects on their demeanor and tolerance of that person. Would you be willing to go out with someone if they were extremely overweight, or intensely thin? Why should the weight or size of a person even become a *mediating* factor in your decision? Our choices should be based on the inner person, not outer appearance. Sound words, but we are all aware that this is not always the case.

There is one common statement made during counseling of many, regardless of gender; that if they were with someone that was seriously overweight, or not so good looking, then they do not fear that the other person would leave them so easily. My position is not to judge, but to guide others by counseling them to a higher understanding of themselves. But the reap benefit from these discussions, we must ask the hard question; How could any person feel so little compassion for their mate, and possess so little self-esteem? If true love exists, then the outward appearance of a person is not all that is seen by the heart of the other.

Couples that stay in bad relationships seem to have common characteristics, in that one partner has exerted so much control over the other that a new way, or a way out, seems to be an impossible dream. The abused person has allowed themselves to be stripped of their belief in themselves. They are not only victims of physical or mental abuse from others, but they are abusing themselves as well. They have allowed someone else to impose upon them a negative interpretation of their self-worth.

It seems to be so easy for anyone who has never experienced an abusive relationship to give advice. The people who think it should be so easy to just walk away and start over. I think we can all agree that no one should stay in an abusive relationship, but there is more to this situation that just relocating, or removing oneself from the exposure of the abuse. So many life factors have been set in motion most feel that they just can't leave, or they fear what they would need to give up.

Most physically abusive relationships become abusive only after a tremendous amount of mental manipulation. Removing yourself from the situation is just the beginning. An abused person has been placed in a situation where their logic of life and truth no longer has meaning. In most cases, the physical abuse begins at the point in which the mental manipulation is no longer effective. The abused person may outwardly believe that they can't do better, but in their hearts, they know that their situation is intolerable.

Anyone that has suffered from abuse may have convinced themselves that this is what they deserve. They may believe that no one else would want them. In these cases, they not only bear the scars of the physical abuse but of the mental abuse as well.

How many times can we use the excuse that "we love them" to inwardly justify the suffering that we feel? Is this truly our version of what love is supposed to be? How many times have you made the below excuses or ask yourself the following questions?

- If I stay with them, maybe they will change.
- I believe they are sorry for what they did.
- If they loved me, then how could they hurt me this way?
- I feel sorry for them, and I don't want to leave them alone.
- What can I do to change my life situation?
- What can I do to change the other person?

If you say "yes" to any of the above, then you need to examine your life in its entirety, and what is to become of it.

Life and love are hard enough even if you have someone that is closely compatible. If you are in an abusive relationship, then your compatibility with this person is shot to hell. Seldom will the abusive behavior stop, and you may be creating your personal "hell on earth".

There is hope for you, as well as for all of mankind. But first, we must consider our value structure and believe that hope does exist. No one is saying that the right-road for you will be an easy one. Quite to the contrary! In many cases the road to recovery is very hard and often must be traveled alone. Just try to remember that it's the hard roads that reap the greatest rewards. Taking the seemingly easy way in life will get you nowhere, the years will merely drift by with no progress. If being happy and successful in life was easy, more people would be in that position.

Chapter 11 - Our Inner Rage

Let us first examine the term "rage", how it differs from anger, and better understand how Rage exhibits traits which can be far more destructive.

Anger is the feeling or emotion itself that a person senses when they are treated badly or even offended by another, and the level of Anger felt is most often determined by the severity felt for the wrongdoing. Anger is more of a mental characteristic not always externally expressed or projected physically onto others. A person can be angry without feeling Rage, but Rage will always have an element of Anger.

Rage is an extreme expression of Anger. Rage is often viewed as the physical action brought on in retaliation to the Anger felt which has built to an uncontrollable level. Anger can be expressed both inwardly and onto others without resulting in physical harm. In many ways, expressing one's Anger can be mentally healthy. Conversely, Rage is an extreme expression of Anger and often results in physical harm. An angry person will most often have control over the emotion, but a person exhibiting Rage can seldom control their actions. Once a person is enraged, their cognizant reasoning is overwhelmed with primal emotions like fear, desperation, and panic, so lashing out at others is often the result. With this clarification presented, let's discuss how anger and rage can affect our lives.

It is all too easy to place blame on another person. Likely we have all done this at one time or another. We can become so enraged that we lash-out and may take out our frustration on others. Our self-control decreases to a point of nonexistent, allowing anger or rage to take over, building up inside to a point where our wrath ignites. In many ways, you may love this person, but under the influences of Cold Love, things may be said or something physical happens that can't be taken back or undone. Cold Love thrives on these types of negative situations, and under its control, you may not care who gets hurt or to what degree.

When someone causes harm to us, be it physical or mental, we may initially focus on their actions alone. Then at some point in time, we start to question what we may have done to deserve such treatment. What caused the other person to present such negative actions towards you, or what set them off?

To properly address the overall problem, we must resolve the issue and truthfully determine the cause. Are we blameless, an innocent victim, a victim exclusively of other's actions? Is it even remotely possible that this was a self-inflicted dilemma which may present culpability on us?

What we seldom ask ourselves is; "why is it that this person has said a certain thing, or done something a certain way"? What caused this form of interaction? Why are they being so hateful, overly aggressive, or defensive? Have you considered that the other person may be reacting to a situation that they do not understand? Once all perspectives are considered, it may present a catch-22 situation, in that no one person is responsible for, and both parties should be held culpable.

Regardless of the nature of the conflict, there are always at least two sides to any situation, and most of the time there may not be one side that is more-right or mostly wrong. Both sides may have merit, or neither grounded in reality.

Couples may argue for hours, or even days causing additional harm, saying hurt-filled things that they don't necessarily mean, or opening up old wounds from the past that were never resolved. It's possible that after some time passing, the couple may forget what initially sparked off the latest argument. Research has determined that few couples will allow a huge argument to occur over a singular topic or issue unless that issue is extreme. The patterns show that the topic that started the argument in question may have simply acted as the catalyst. In truth, these confrontations are most often caused by a build-up of unresolved issues over time, an accumulation of many issues masked inside of a person, not discussed for many days, weeks or even years.

Very often when we suppress our fears and anger, we allow things to build to an eruption of emotions that even we cannot sort out or control. When this form of emotions manifest itself, we feel somewhat absent of a true understanding, our judgment becomes clouded in doubt. When these built-up emotions finally erupt, we may not necessarily be reacting to the present-day issue or what appears to be the catalyst.

While in a heated discussion or argument with your mate, do you find yourself thinking only of a comment to counter something that they said, or reacting only to the major points that you want to cover? This causes further disconnect. In retrospect, do you realize that you were not listening to all that was being said? This may be occurring on both sides of the conversation, so both parties dig themselves deeper into the preverbal hole, with no resolution reached beyond the ending of the discussion, for now. By the time you separate yourself from the argument, things appear only worse than before. You are left feeling more alone, more doubtful.

We seem to have become experts at dodging the true issues at hand, as our mind shifts into the defensive mode quickly. In this particular mode, we are self-consumed, often only searching for our justifications. Very little attention or sympathy is offered to our partner. We hear although we do not listen. We look but do not see.

During these arguments, do you have a sense that for each word spoken the fear of full disclosure looms? What are you hiding? Is your partner reacting in the same manner? With so many emotions flooding through our thoughts, with so much self-doubt and honesty being concealed within our words and actions, it's a wonder that any relationships are reconciled. Uncertainty becomes abundant, and our inner-security suffers.

While engaged within an argument, and the more insecure we feel with this person, the more intent we seem to be in winning this battle of relationship positioning. We feel that we must come out on top in order of our self-defense, or to retain our self-worth. We seldom see that if we could only muster some consideration and understanding for the other person, both would benefit in the long run, and the situation would cool off much quicker. Perhaps even bringing you both closer.

At those times within a disagreement, if the truth were allowed within our cognizant understanding, allowing total honesty within ourselves, then we may see that our version of winning an argument is often self-serving, and can be self-deceiving. Even if it appears that we have won the argument, we most often walk away with a hollow trophy, not feeling any degree of personal growth.

Are you in a relationship that allows you to express yourself freely, totally open and honest? Not just honest with the other person, but honest with yourself. If not, then how is it that you decided to relinquish your opinions, stifling the true you, to renounce your claim as an individual, resign from your beliefs. Giving up on that special person that only you can attain is a forfeiture to all. What accomplishments may be lost to this world for your un-giving?

Each of us is worthy of the opportunity to express our individuality. This is our God-given right and responsibility. If you cannot be free emotionally, then question yourself as to why. Within many examined relationships, what was never expressed was far more destructive than the more often-spoken misguided words. Why allow anger and rage an opportunity to destroy what was built, what you want in life?

To help bring out a better you, surround yourself with others that are of like mind and care for you unselfishly. People who support you when you are right or help to guide you back to your true path when you stray. Place yourself within situations that allow for personal freedom and growth. If you find it hard to be open and honest with the people around you, perhaps you may need to reevaluate both your method of seeking interactions and the people you share your time with. How will you grow as a person if you stifle your true self?

Within some interactions, people will often mold their conversations to a self-serving goal. Similar to a con-artist, who often speaks in the form of a psychological manipulator. The great pretenders! These are often the friendliest of people to meet and openly talk with, as they have conditioned themselves to be this way. If you allow them to be close to you, and once they accomplish their goal, you may be left empty-handed and full of rage because you allowed yourself to care for them. Be on guard, as Cold Love exist in abundance and often cloaked.

Are we so lost in our self-doubt that others cause us to be so preventive, so guarded? What are we sheltering? What are we trying to rationalize? What lies deep within us that is so obscure or hurt filled that we can't face it? On the surface, one may think that this form of verbal self-manipulation stems from distrust of others, and to some point this fact holds. Still the hard question to ask is, "why are we so distrustful of ourselves"?

As individuals, no one can know us as well as we know ourselves. Within us, lies answers to questions we could only pose to ourselves. Inner wisdom that we are not always open to or aware of. No other person could be so open to the understanding that we require.

The truth of the matter is, everyone has a bit of a dark side, even ever so slight, contained within their subconscious. To some, it is an obscure voice. For others, it could be their dominate influencer. The plain fact is that there is no justification for projecting our stern views or values onto others, unless you are asked to do so, and only then in a sympathetic manner. If your views and way of life work for you, fine! However, there still exists the question; Is your understanding as clear as it should be?

We may allow ourselves to get so wrapped up in the game playing that we relinquish our true purpose in life. Some may even enjoy the challenge. Some may enjoy this manipulation. OK, play the mind games as you were taught. Pass on this dark wisdom, so out of control, this form of Cold Love. What will it take to brighten your path? If you want to survive, you must calm your inner rage!

Chapter 12 – Self Exploration

Many people at some point in time will make the statement, "put yourself in my shoes". Consider what is being asked very carefully. How would you put yourself in someone's shoes? How could your life and experiences be so similar to this person that would allow you to truly understand their mindset and why they react to situations in certain ways? How could we feel the true emotions that the other person is feeling? How could we know the fears of another? Scary to think about, but until we explore these emotions and understand where they are coming from, we are predestined to descend into the same snare of misunderstanding which plagues many.

Conversely, can we knowingly blind ourselves from the emotions of others? Certainly! At times, people get so wrapped up in their own personal problems they have little-to-no sympathy for others. Some people also isolate themselves from the world around them, consumed by their own personal issues. This type of behavior may often be viewed as the person just being cold-hearted or uncaring. However, we must consider that this person may know little about being raised in a caring environment, having people around who they know truly cares for them, so they withdraw into their version of what is safe, presenting a self-induced shielding to act as their defense mechanism.

It also stands to reason that we must first understand what our own emotional reaction would be if put in a similar situation in order to fully understand others' innermost feelings. This is extremely necessary so that a clear un-diluted view of where someone is coming from can be felt and understood to some degree. It may take practice, but we have the ability to gain a more-true understanding of other people's feelings and why they may be reacting in a doubt-filled manner.

If you attempt this exercise of self-exploration, you may first experience a flood of emotions felt from past conversations or situations within your life experiences scrolling past your inner vision. Some noted accounts of this type of experience are well documented, stating that it is as if a movie of their life is played out before them in just a few seconds. Similar experiences are recorded from trauma patients when they state that their life flashed before them. However, we don't always need to be traumatized to examine or relive our past conversations or events.

In one specific account from a subject that had suffered a traumatic event to their head, they described visions from the past that scrolled by within seconds, yet the recounted visions did not stop on that specific day. As the visions began to diminish, the subject claimed that sporadic occurrences, snapshots of events, went several days into the future. This subject claimed to have suffered many hours as he relived these periodic feelings, desahvue. Although these accounts have no scientific manner available to test or confirm, it is only mentioned herein to stress the importance of what our minds are capable of if we can present the level of focus required.

If we truly want to better understand ourselves and others, we must practice focusing our minds. We must first learn to focus our inner sight, as a camera would focus on a subject. Initially, once a topic is chosen, your mind may quickly attempt a conclusion, trying to fool you into breaking away from the journey. Move past that urge as quickly as possible. If you had resolved the issue previously, it would not likely be a topic brought forward during this exercise. Continue, and attempt to view the undesirable issue from a different perspective.

If your main focus is something that someone did to harm you, your mind will want to pass a quick judgment, perhaps as before, or to just move on. Your inner thoughts may try to convince you that this additional effort is not worth your time. At times, our minds are so quick to conclude that we were the victim, nothing more. Part of this reevaluation is to find hope, renew our inner strength, to move past our old conclusions, to not see ourselves as victims, and to allow a new beginning. To gain the most benefit from our new effort, we must allow new considerations, and most importantly, allow forgiveness.

We must forgive others for the suffering created in our life, if only for a moment during our self-reexamination exercises. Like all unwanted things in our life, we may need the baby-steps to get us started toward our end goal. We must also forgive ourselves for the infestation allowed into our version of the event, causing us to hate or be regretful, which is creating self-torment. This self-destructive form of harsh judgment that is blinding us, and will not allow our true nature to see or feel that which is truer. Caution must be present to not allow self-righteousness to prevent this unveiling of the true self.

We must first take this journey inside of our understanding. It is imperative that we let down our guard and allow a new more sympathetic viewpoint. It is now that we must face ourselves, our demons. Only then can we see past our barriers of rationalization, and only then will raw truth unveil itself.

Let us begin. You must find a place of solitude. A place without distractions that you feel comfortable and relaxed.

Sitting very quietly and alone with yourself, close your eyes. Breath at a steady rhythmic pace. See yourself as calm and peaceful. Imagine yourself living in a world in which you may express yourself freely, without any fear of condemnation. A world where truth outweighs the fear of condemnation and compassion is rewarded with forgiveness.

Now, very gently place yourself in the situation that may be troubling you. Try to envision the situation as if you were a spectator, not as a participant. Do not allow any distressing feelings within, as your version of a troubling moment or situation is recalled. Remember that you were there, but your version was jaded by your intrusive self-defense mechanism. You must place yourself in the position of a mediator, mentally listening to both sides of the argument or situation.

If you find yourself recalling things that were said to you that before you could not recall, then you have pressed pass a mental barrier that allowed you to listen even while you were speaking. Things that were never before taken into consideration.

Envision yourself listening, calm and relaxed, recount the comments that were exchanged. Hear the retorts back and forth, and question what new outcomes could have been found if handled differently. As this new form of understanding takes place, envision yourself as the other party, try to "put yourself in their shoes". View through their eyes, hear from their perspective.
Can you now better understand the attitude that you once projected onto them, or better react to the comments they made to you? Do you feel the psychological attachment that the other person must have felt from their viewpoint? Feel their understanding of this situation. Try to comprehend their version of why they felt right in their actions.

Are you now as right as once believed? Can you now see yourself not as a victim nor as the bad guy, only as a person trying to deal with inner truth? See the situation, re-think what was said, hear with your new understanding, think of what should have been said. What would have been the result if only a few kind words had been spoken? Debating who said, or did, what initially is like arguing the chicken and the egg quandary, the end result is insensible resulting is nothing positive.

You alone can account for the events leading up to these situations, how things were handled, but you can only know your version of the truth. The truth is not always that skewed version set forth in your verbal reiteration to others. That version told so many times that your subconscious is starting to believe. It is, however, a universal truth that it is seldom a matter of who was more right or wrong, but it is always most important how we handled the situations. One true value that the past contains is wisdom. Wisdom awaiting your understanding.

Continue this journey as you now start implanting memories of others, what you know about them, and allowing their life experiences to further mold your understanding of that person. You must feel compassion for others. Everyone has their own battles to fight, and they may be suffering in this life, as much as you have.

If we don't allow our innermost self to evolve, then our journey through this life can be analogous to the lamb being led to slaughter. We can't simply follow our instincts with blind devotion. Human instincts are similar to that of animals, both having genetically hard-wired behaviors that are meant to enhance our ability to cope with dynamic environmental stimuli or conditions, not to dominate our daily decisions. Understanding that mankind's basic instincts, including denial, revenge, greed, and proliferation, will soon threaten our very existence.

Do you want to be just another person adding to the problem, or to help yourself to enjoy this life to a higher degree? We must understand that most instincts are hereditary and often unforgiving. Our instincts do not encompass calm reasoning. It is our behavior that is facilitated by reactions often deep within our subconscious.

With this self-exploration of our inner sight, we become more open to the understanding of how others see us. If we can, for only seconds, sense the emotions that we project onto others, we will dilute the quick conclusions in our understanding of life. We become more open-minded, and receptive to true wisdom.

Do we truly know and understand the emotions that we exhibit in our everyday life? If not this, then why not that? Is what we see or hear truly what is being presented to us? Is our interpretation of the situation so jaded and skewed that we appear, "out of it", by others?

We as individuals comprehend in a very unique way. We may differ from others, but we are indeed different from others. One must truly understand that we can never totally see things the way someone else does. We are looking out while others are attempting to look in.

In this exercise of mental melting, we may hope to transverse other's paths of understanding. In this way, we may better understand how others perceive us. Within this exploration of self, questions should arise about our perceptions. If we can question our deliberation, then our boundaries have grown. We will gain a greater understanding of ourselves and mankind as a whole. As we consider this lifting of limitations, then we grow as a greater self.

If after your journey you have gained a truer understanding of yourself, then life begins renewed. By gaining a truer understanding of self, we can more fully understand others and our effect on them. If we have to go to such lengths to block out our brainwashing of ourselves, then let us further understand the mental manipulation that we put others through. Let us use our great knowledge and compassion. Allow ourselves to grow.

Chapter 13 - Do We Need Cold Love

Ask yourself this question very carefully; Do we need Cold Love? As posed, your first reaction may be a hasty;" NO"! OK, then why do we at times seek it out, or allow this form of love into our lives? Entering into a relationship should be a cognizant action, but many will fall for someone without truly knowing them. As with all things in life, our actions have consequences. Getting involved with someone you barely know is akin to opening the door to a stranger. Why do we sometimes seek out or offer invitations to a form of love that consumes more than it offers? In this world of uncertainties, do we really need this psychological form of expression that pushes our physical and mental being to the boundaries of self-abuse?

At times, people often feel so alone and desperate for affection that they do things that later are regretful. This doesn't make them a bad person, but it should cause anyone to pause and think about the reasons why we do what we do. How much time have you spent alone over the past few months, or at least felt alone?

Loneliness can present a form of subliminal desperation, causing us to let our guard down. There are times when we will allow Cold Love to enter into our lives, perhaps against your better judgment, in an effort to fill that aching void within, similar to a conciliation to not being able to find your envisioned partner. We may feel so lost that we are willing to settle for far less than our standards would normally permit. This form of hooking-up will seldom go the distance or work out in the long-term. All that we achieve is a short-term gratification by filling a large void with a shallow hope. When entering into a relationship under these circumstances we are not only inviting Cold Love into our lives, we are presenting Cold Love as well. A true recipe for disaster.

When we ask ourselves, "do we need Cold Love?", how can we answer with any certainty? What if, by experiencing Cold Love we are teaching ourselves the way to find true happiness, or at least a better understanding of what we don't want? Is this the right road to our finding happiness, or are we *derailing* that quest?

At any point in time have you considered giving up on your search for true love? Time after time you invest so much of yourself only to be disappointed. Can you recall that within each relationship you entered into, your wants and needs appear to change, at least to some degree? This is caused by our day-to-day living and experiencing life. What may have satisfied us a year ago may not be sufficient today because we are not the same as we were a year ago. Time changes us as we mature. To some degree, we may not truly realize what will make us happy long-term. Most of us are only sure about what doesn't work at a particular time in our life.

A great mind once inscribed that, "what's right, is what's left, after everything else that you have tried has been wrong". For most, this view is not at all reassuring. To accept this analogy, we must embrace the fact that we may suffer through several situations before we find our true self or our true love. We will have to see ourselves as willing participants in this process of elimination.

Can you feel the difference between a love that is right, and that which is wrong? At this point, have you realized that something is very inappropriate with the relationship that you have involved yourself with? Is it your intention to continue this veiling of truth? Not only of others but yourself as well.

Perhaps you could be more content if you did not stir such an evaluation of yourself. Just the thought that we could be so cold to ourselves or others, is disheartening. What need are we trying to fulfill?

Does your partner feel the same way? Maybe you do not want to know. Is it easier to go through life wearing blinders, not realistically dealing with what is the truth? Always being an unwilling victim, or unknowingly victimizing others? Living in a self-proclaimed hell? How will you deal with the truth?

Can you look at yourself in the mirror and like all that you see? Is that part of you that is your inner spiritual being holding onto the past, or hoping for the future? Once we realize what long term influence that Cold Love relationships breed, I am not sure that we will be so quick to engage in its role-playing.

If in fact, Cold Love can reveal that inner self that we do not wish to contain, then has it not served a purpose? Can we not learn from this dark wisdom? Is it not true, that when we know of that which is harmful to us, we may gain the power in which to conquer it?

Perhaps Cold Love has always been a part of the grand design, to be a part of our natural evolution. To evolve, we must grow and change. If we were born into a world of pure love and goodness, then what would motivate our need for growth or change? If happiness and contentment were in overabundance throughout our lives, then what would inspire our determination?

If there is in fact a true need for Cold Love in our daily lives, we can only hope that we can acquire some control over it. It would be of great benefit to mankind if we would allow the good from within us to overcome the effects that Cold Love propagates.

Cold Love can be present not just in a marriage or a friendship, but in a dating relationship as well. Cold Love has no boundaries other than what we establish. It exists in families and throughout society. Cold Love can be seen within any one person whose selfishness governs their personality. That one person who says or even thinks to themselves; "I can do whatever I want to whomever I please". They often want things to occur only their way, not wavering or flexible, stating that no one has the right to tell them what to do. They think they can control others and they always need to be in total control. They often take the position that people should accept them as they are and they do not need to change themselves.

A person allowing Cold Love to dominate their life is often afraid of commitments. They present many promises, but often those same promises are short-lived. If a commitment was true it could not be discarded easily, similar to true love itself. Even in cases where a couple feels that they are in love, if the commitment is not there then that same level of love can be taken away.

Some couples may seemingly commit for a short period of time, but as soon as that pseudo-commitment ends so does the love they once felt. This is not true love, nor a true commitment, only further evidence that Cold Love exist.

A true commitment is a result of true love and unity. Without these qualities, people often give-up, they quit the relationship even when they at first felt sensitivity, affection, kindness, and tenderness. Their compassion soon fades eventually dying off as selfishness takes over. The great deceiver, Cold Love, has worked its black magic.

Chapter 14 - Indicators of Cold Love

Cold Love may appear as passion as it is passed between lovers, often disguised as an intense wanting or need. If you find yourself trying harder and harder at passion, waiting for that certain level of self-satisfaction, then think about what is going on inside of yourself.

Does your heart want to hold this person dearly, to commit, or do you just want to push away? What feelings arise when you hold this person close? Are those hugs and kisses enough to hold you over for a few hours? Do you remember a different relationship when you could kiss for hours and feel the warmth of love, even without the sexual bonding? That time in your life when just being in love with this person made you feel like royalty. Is it possible to get close to this person, without having to be intimate?

Do you question your reasoning as to why you are with your current partner? In what ways do you feel truly connected to them? Is there a bond, or are you just together?

Very often relationships spring out of a personal need to be fulfilled, or a wanting to be a part of something more. Have you asked yourself lately, "what would I do if I lost this person"? Would you just move on to another so easily?

If you are seeking answers as to "how to maintain a long-term relationship", then it's likely you are either on that razor-edge of a break-up or perhaps trying to correct the mistakes made within a previous relationship. If at this point you do not take the time to truly evaluate your inner quandaries, your understanding of true love, then you may soon lose a part of yourself that may take you years to recover, if at all.

You must ask yourself, "Do I need this specific person, or just need someone to be close to"? Is it that your inner desires are causing you to rationalize the situation just to fulfill an immediate need or a self-serving conclusion?

When all consideration is given to your current relationship, taking all facts into consideration, do you *interpret* your reasoning objectively, or are you *rationalizing*? Have you considered ending the relationship before now? Is there a worthwhile reason for continuing the relationship? Have you compromised your desires for a short-term solution? It may be true that life is filled with tradeoffs, but it is also true that our actions must be accounted for.

When you look at this person, how many things concerning their physical appearance would you like to change? Or is it that their personality is not compatible with yours? Do you often wish that they were a bit more intelligent, or more of an intellectual? Perhaps they are of high-brow character causing you to question your place in the overall order of things?

Do you spend time as a couple? Perhaps, you have your friends, and they have their own, yet you seldom find common ground for everyone to be together? What do your friends say concerning your mate or partner? What do your mate's friends think about you? Would you more strongly consider staying or leaving the relationship, on the advice of your friends?

Do your friends help in your certainty of the relationship, or is it more self-assurance that keeps you going? Are you secure in your heart that this person loves you for the right reasons?

Do you feel a sense of pride when you are with your mate? If so, pride for what reason? Are you satisfying your hunger for love, and to be loved? Is there a part of you that feels empty, and wanting for more? Do you see other couples that appear to be happy, and feel sad for what you may be missing? What is this part of you that fails to be content? Are you living your life, or dwelling in another's *conceptual dominion*?

Is what you feel outward, or express to others, truly the way you feel towards your mate, or are you trying so hard to convince yourself that you are happy? Are you willingly inching towards that preverbal "edge of the cliff"? Remind yourself of a real love that you have known in your life, and compare those emotions with what you feel today. If it doesn't measure up then Cold Love may exist. True Love can be an amazing experience when you find yourself being happy for seemingly no particular reason, and not having to try so hard.

Cold Love is not always easy to recognize in a relationship. It is sometimes so silent even a whisper of hope can drown out its presence. Attempting to appease your desires by allowing Cold Love in a relationship is like trying to fill a bottomless pit in your soul. True Love gives all. Cold Love is a deceiver that offers much then devours hope.

Chapter 15 - How Do We End Cold Love

Grounded from the perspective that we are attempting to clarify here, trying to end Cold Love entirely may be an impossible task. That effort is comparable to trying to end evil as we understand it. However, we do have the ability to diminish the effects that Cold Love may present on our lives. First, we must realize that we have little control over the natural laws between cause and effect. However, if we want to enact change then we must address the root-cause of things. Once the cause is addressed, the alternate and corresponding effect will alter naturally, hopefully in a more positive way.

Our first hope should be that we can just survive the experience. Cold Love can be one of the most brutal forms of emotion that a relationship has to offer, or a person could give. Cold Love can be so intense, so masked, that you never knew what hit you until it's too late. Not intense in a warm way, but in a fearful way.

Let us now consider a different viewpoint. Our everyday fears of the unknown or misunderstood presents to us that life is full of obstacles. Do we question whether these obstacles were purposely placed to prevent us from finding our true path, or to steer us toward it? What feelings would replace apprehension if we could determine the results of our actions before we act?

Perhaps what builds in a Cold Love relationship is a desire to overcome the obstacles. To break through the barriers placed in our way by someone without forethought or compassion. We may conclude that these barriers are preventing us from feeling real love for someone and blinding us to what is the truth. But, how correct may our assumptions be? Is something preventing you from seeing what is best for you, or have you allowed Cold Love to shadow your emotions? What, or who caused it?

No one could claim that we can put an end to Cold Love, but I do believe that we can diminish its effects on our lives, and the hold it can have on us. Our offensive stance toward Cold Love's consequence serves as our resistance to its wrongful self-righteousness.

Some other ways that we may diminish the hold that Cold Love has placed in our lives is to consider even the smallest detail that affirms its grip on us. See things for what they are, not for what you want them to be.

You know that when you plant a seed you expect something to grow. When people lie, mislead, or deceive others, they plant seeds of harmful intent. What form of manifestation do we expect to arise from these seeds? Lies will break down a relationship and shatter all faith and trust faster than anything else known, and yes cheating is a lie also. Lies break apart our lives into hundreds of fragments that no longer make any sense. Before we realize what is going on, we have pieces of our life's puzzle that will not fit together nicely. In time, if left unchecked, our life-puzzle becomes more like numerous different puzzles mixed, or seems as if we have unintentionally thrown some of the vital pieces away. How can we ever hope to solve the puzzle that is the US we seek?

Almost all of us have attempted to solve a large puzzle of some sort in our lifetime. Remember the disappointment that you felt when in the end some of the pieces were missing, or amid this quandary, nothing appeared to fit. What is inside of us, that makes this conquering so important? The need to make sense of all of the mental pieces which dwell inside? This urge appears to be a similar desire in all people whom try to live a prosperous life. In many ways, we feel threatened by the uncertainty created, that lost feeling of non-completion.

Now let us make this connection to our relationships. Cold Love is very menacing to our inner-self, our faith. Most often misunderstood, yet so powerful as to hold a steal grip on us. Cold Love needs our mistrust of ourselves, and of others. Once you have allowed Cold Love into your understanding, we cannot just walk away from its influences.

For some, Cold Love can become an addiction. To some degree, a person can appear to be possessed by Cold Love's power over others. The ability to manipulate others can be known by many, as we are all aware. Most have known that person who chooses to take what they want, only to serve or fulfill their desires.

Anyone may be consumed by Cold Love's intensity, if they chose to dwell in this dark realm, no one is immune. No one person holds the key to renounce Cold Love's consequences. There is no one answer to the problems that afflict so many. Cold Love is a chameleon, presenting unique personalities governed by each individual's traits and misdeeds.

Our only hope as individuals is that our understanding of how we interact with others will breed wisdom and intelligence for future reference. We must understand that if we want a brighter future then we must allow ourselves to be open to the significance of truth and honesty.

A person experiencing the effects of Cold Love feels an inner hurt and a sense of *demoralization*. Something inside has been taken away. No, not some kind of love that someone else took from them. A more proper analogy would be that something inside has become so scared and battered that it may take some time for its wound to heal, although the scars will remain. Anyone with a heart is susceptible to stumbling into a relationship ruled by Cold Love if they let their guard down.

How do we end this immorality to one's self? How do we cope with the loss of our true self? We sometimes feel that we must place blame on someone for this inhumane reality that we are enduring. We are not frequently empowered mentally to deal with this rage that dwells inside of us.

We try, but we cannot continuously hide our hurt, it projects around us in every direction. On some occasions, people feel that the guilty party, or the person that they are attempting to blame for their situation, should not be allowed to live. They truly believe that if this person is not allowed to hurt again, this will somehow make them feel better. Have they convinced themselves that this person has used another human without remorse, or perhaps it is that they are hurting so much inside because they fear that the guilty party may find some sort of happiness that is undeserving to them? Do we fully understand what happens within us when we summon so much hate for someone?

Some believe that when we hate with such intensity, our thought waves may be projected from our presence. It is also believed that many of us can direct these energies. This hypothesis concludes that if we focus our anger toward an individual that great harm may come to them. The same doctrine further states that if we do not focus this energy, it can be unleashed without direction or purpose which can backfire or hurt an innocent person.

When this form of energy is so misdirected, it may strike at will, anywhere it pleases. It can turn on an innocent party, or even become a self-inflicted curse. The doctrine coincides with this form of misdirected energy to the manifestation of freak-accidents. Many have witnessed such occurrences, but few have been explained with any degree of certainty.

The only solution would be to conquer this apparition of Cold Love that dwells within us. We must allow our understanding to evolve to a new level. We must appraise the consequences left behind and to come. We must consider not only our actions but our inaction as well. If we so desire a more-pure understanding of ourselves and others then this must be our sacrament. Our obligation to this world, our children, and to all that we hold dear.

Chapter 16 - Understanding Emotional Pain

At that time when we feel we are at a low mental state in our life, we should stop for a moment and contemplate the lingering pain that exists within us. One of the worse aspects of ending a relationship is the lingering negative thoughts left behind for us to deal with. Thoughts of bitterness perhaps, that which is allowed to consume our memories and perpetuate our mental anguish. The type of hurt that is continuous and does not dissipate in a short amount of time. A person may go for months, or even years, carrying around the haunting memories of all lies told, the mental anguish inflicted upon them, or worse, and having to deal with physical harm imposed upon them.

Physical pain is easier to understand, as the cause is often very clear and to some degree easier to guard against. Most understand that physical pain has the ability to create emotional pain, but few are aware that emotional pain can cause physical harm to your body if left unresolved. When we allow the continual bombardment of emotional pain within our minds, chemical changes occur. These changes can range from a minor mental set-back to other significant symptoms which can be debilitating if left unchecked, affecting your overall physical health and well-being.

For those who have suffered through an intense emotional period, it was made very clear that emotional pain can cause physical harm. Some become so distraught they begin choking and breathing erratically, often making them feel drained of energy, lethargic, and reporting sore limbs and joints.

Others report that their emotional pain made them feel very angry, that their muscles would tense-up and their breathing became rapid and labored. This is caused by the brain releasing large amounts of adrenaline. Their anxiety levels increase, which hampers their ability to relax. Some report symptoms of nausea and other stomach disorders. If the anger is not expressed or relieved in some manner, the adrenaline levels can cause long-term stress-tension or even develop into an outburst of rage.

Emotional pain affects our thoughts, feeling and behaviors, often caused by our frustrated psychological needs. Needs that relate to our desire to love or to be loved, our desire to be self-sufficient, our wanting to fit-in or to be a part of something greater than ourselves, our need to feel achievement, or our need to avoid harm, shame or embarrassment.

Emotional or psychological pain can reduce our fitness for survival, and is often expressed when someone becomes grief-stricken or heartbroken, causing them to feel anguish, torment, alone and distressed. Some attempt to relieve the intensity of this pain by crying hysterically, while others may choose to lash out at anyone who is readily accessible. Emotional pain will often cause a person's self-worth to diminish, and allow them to question if life is truly tolerable.

If left unresolved, a person can become so totally self-absorbed they ignore the harm they may be causing to others. In an attempt at relief, they lash out, inflicting their mental pain onto others without any thought of what they are doing or the damage they may be causing. "Misery loves company" is more than a proverbial adage.

In a relationship where Cold Love exists, there can be a high degree of mental pain inflected upon, and experienced by, each person involved. In some cases, perhaps the lies and pain are being presented by one person, while in other cases by both persons. One, or both, may seem to care little about the harm they inflict on others or upon themselves. An eye for an eye perhaps? Are we to punish all because we were hurt? These are the traits present within the givers and receivers of Cold Love.

Like many others, you want to trust the people around you. You want your love to account for something. Perhaps you care for someone that may not know how to love purely, having no true love within them for you. If the person that you love is a giver of Cold Love, then your life desires or goals may never be obtained. Your understanding of what love and relationships should be may become shadowed in disbelief.

After the trust is lost. After the hope of true love is tarnished. After the truth is haunting your dreams of how you allowed someone to use you in such a manner. How do you deal with yourself? Knowing that if you had been truer to yourself, then you would never have allowed this person to treat you that way. Recovery is often a lonely road, and at times a long journey, but there is hope within us. Giving up is not a viable option.

Regardless of how much harm Cold Love has caused in your life, you have to find a new meaning. You have to find a new part of yourself to fill this void that the absent partner or loss has left within you. If at about this time in the reading this book, during your recovery effort, someone new comes into your life, and you allow them to temporarily fill that void, well, I will see you again in a few months. The only advice I can offer at this time is; "Don't jump back into another relationship with the unresolved hurt left behind from your past issues".

No! You are still here! Good for you! Never try to allow another person to fill that void inside you. It cannot be done. Self-worth, your happiness, cannot be found within others.

Only you can find your happiness. Do not fool yourself, or rationalize the situation. Do not hide in another's emotions. That may have been the reasoning that got you into trouble in your past relationship. Trying to just "fill the void" is the type of attitude that attracts the wrong type of person for you. The "user of others" can sense your loneliness or desperation, and are attracted to you like a moth to a flame.

What do we mean when we say, "attract the wrong type of person or personality"? Let us examine how our present outlook and attitudes may present an altered personality, and how this may be looked upon as, "who we truly are".

When we feel alone, we sometimes think too much about the negatives. Perhaps we feel as if we need to punish ourselves to bring about some form of forgiveness. In reality, you should be forgiving yourself and try to build a more enlightened person inside of yourself.

Our harmful thoughts can drive our self-esteem to depths never before known and cause us to become a different person, altering our true personality. When this *metamorphosis* has taken place, you will often react to situations in a manner that does not reflect your true self. If this mind-set continues over a prolonged period, you may lose the inner-self you once knew, then *apprehension* sets in. Your negative actions or lack of positive thoughts could cause your entire life to spiral out of control.

What has happened to that inner person that you once knew and loved? It may seem as if a cloud has cast a shadow over the goodness that you once felt. You may find yourself overcompensating in your efforts just to deal with everyday life. You may have plagued yourself with anxiety and doubt to the point where you can't think intelligently.

Do you remember the saying, "Oh what a tangled web we weave"? Well, then what about the deceiving of ourselves? Would you lower your standards and allow someone into your life just to stop the loneliness? And, if it was the loneliness that you feared most, perhaps that which drove you into the last relationship, then why didn't it subside once you entered into the new relationship? Short-term gratification may be evident at first, but if you're not in the right type of relationship that best serves you, then a vicious circle begins.

Perhaps now you began to feel a different form of mental pain. The pain of being involved with someone for all of the wrong reasons. The pain of being with someone so different than what you truly want.

Let's assume for a moment that things are better now in this new relationship, and you are going through a lot of mental changes. Then as the weeks pass, this relationship starts to grow cold and distant. Your outlook on this new relationship turns to fear. You try to mask it, but mentally you may change to such a degree that you are not the same person that your partner fell in love with. Your feelings about yourself and for this new person in your life has taken a major turn. The love that you felt before, where did it go? Was it love, or was it need? Was it love you felt or was it, Cold Love? Harboring Cold Love, no matter how deep you try to hide it away, may cause problems in any future relationship you attempt.

No one can predict how a relationship will evolve. But one thing is for certain. If we don't take the time to understand how Cold Love can blind us and obscure our inner vision, we may live out our entire adult life bouncing in and out of relationships.

If you now end the relationship trying to save yourself, you may feel as if you are back to the point at which you started, alone. However! Try to consider that you are not alone, you are now free with your thoughts. Reflect on past mistakes and gain the wisdom that they contain. Your truth is within you alone, and only you can find your happiness. Remember the movie "Groundhog Day"? Will you continue to relive the same or similar circumstances forever, or until you get it "right"? Right being defined as; doing the right things for the right reasons.

What about the other person? What devastation have you left behind? They may have truly loved you. The person that they fell in love with may have been just what they needed in their life. Stop, think about, "what they needed"! That is the assumption that you were under as well. Was their need as much a form of Cold Love as your own?

We may hope that the other party was as misdirected as we were. In some ways, it helps in coping with the separation. It allows some justification for the hurt that we feel or may have caused.

Can you now more clearly see, that when you are no longer "yourself", you are indeed attracting the wrong type of personality for you? Stop and consider what you want, and stop falling victim to what will satisfy some short-term yearning. Think over what you hope to accomplish in the long run. Something that will truly make you happy.

Can you now see and understand more clearly how mental pain affects our understanding? Not just the pain inflected upon ourselves, but the pain that we may inflict on others.

Chapter 17 - Responsibilities in a Relationship

Are you a responsible person? Are you doing your part to make your relationship work? There are at least two parties in any form of relationship, with each person having responsibilities that may not be fully understood.

If you were involved in a relationship that lacked a desirable level of honesty, is that what you wanted? Do you want to sit up at night wondering where your partner is, or what they are doing? How does it make you feel to make plans for the afternoon just to find yourself sitting and waiting for them to show up? They may not only not show up, but you may not even receive a phone call explaining why. In many relationships, you will find this type of behavior abundant.

When some enter into a relationship, they often consider that; "this is meant to be", or that they have found their soul mate. They consider that they have found the kind of love that will carry them through to the remainder of their days. For the first few weeks, they seemed to have lengthy conversations and enjoyed being together. Both are enjoying it to the point that they decide to move in together, only after knowing each other for such a short time. At first, they speak openly and caring to each other, and expressing concerns about honesty in a relationship, and how important open communication is to them. But after a few weeks, maybe months, they start to stray away from the intimacy. They try to talk and work out the problem, but nothing appears to be getting through. They express that they care for each other and they don't want to give up on the relationship. What happened?

Often, we find ourselves saying something because we think it is what the other person wants to hear, but in reality, we are setting our relationship up to fail, if sincerity doesn't exist. We often find that what a person says is different than what they meant, and it will always hold true that actions speak louder than words.

When one specific case-study couple took an opportunity to talk, they found themselves constantly injecting weird or odd topics into the conversation, so much so that the main points of interest were lost. At least one party conceded that this was purposeful, and meant to throw the other off-track, making it hard to focus or get to any real truth. For this couple, they pushed away from each other, soon only having an opportunity to speak to each other at work, so their time and freedom together to speak openly was limited. Eventually, they agreed to allow each other some space, time to see other people and see if their caring could survive.
They tried to allow their mate an opportunity to run free and possibly get these unexpressed feelings out of their system, but each soon found that having to deal with all of the secrecy was too hard to deal with. While agreeing to this separation, they both clearly stated that if each needed some time to party, or date others, they would understand and try to wait for the other. Yet even this tactic yielded only obscurity, no truthful results, nothing that helped the couple to rekindle what once was.

Trying to fall in love with the wrong person, or for the wrong reasons, can make you a bit blind to the facts-of-life, and at times a bit unwise. When we feel as if we have found the right person to be with, someone to love, someone that may love us, we do tend to overlook the numerous warning signs that pop-up, hoping that we can work through the disconnects. Our inner rationalization attempts to skew or blind us to the facts, as we can only hope that the worst will not happen again. We may even conclude that this person may not be perfect, but we can fix them, alter them to be more like what we want. This type of logic most often fails. There are reasons behind why someone is the way they are and you can't control their inner beliefs, or alter their inner programming. This is not to say that the other person cannot change, but it is a reality that only they have that power over themselves. You can't force a leopard to change its spots.

A person's responsibility in a relationship does not end in just telling someone that they care, in fact, this is when the responsibilities begins. Couples often jump into relationships, declaring "I love you" without truly understanding the commitment they are taking on. If you want someone in your life, and you proclaim your commitment, then you have a moral responsibility to them. An obligation to treat them like a decent human being. An obligation of concern, kindness, and honesty. Often a person expects others to be honest with them, but they cannot see how they are hurting the other with their verbal manipulation of facts. How can one expect truth when they live in lies? Sincerity flourishes in truth, and Cold Love has no grounding within sincerity.

When you tell someone that you will see them at a certain time, that is as much as a promise. The other person expects some validity to what is being said to them. How can a person abandon their promise to another? They talk the talk, then go about whatever else comes along as if they had not made a prior obligation. Do they even so much as consider that someone is waiting for their arrival, and maybe greatly concerned as to what is going on? How can someone give their promise to another, and feel no remorse in breaking that vow?

Is it out of reason to consider that if a person is told something that they have the right to an explanation if the situation does not develop as planned? When plans or promises are made, why should we not expect them to be valid? The person left waiting for a fulfilled promise is at a loss of reasoning as to why they are involved in this situation.

They may have loved the other and want only truth. They cannot consider how anyone could be so cold and heartless, especially when the other claims that they care so much for them. As often experienced, what is promised and what occurs is seldom the same.

It is every individual's right to come and go as they please. But why can't this be done in a way that prevents hurt and anger to others? If a person is not happy in a relationship, then why not express that truth? Allow the other person to deal with the facts. If the truth is presented properly, then both parties can at least keep some form of respect for themselves and for each other, even if the relationship is eventually dissolved.

It now seems to be the way of the world, for individuals to mask their true intentions toward their partners, or to others in general. They think that they can rationalize any situation to fit their own needs. Are they so jaded to true love and what it takes to make a good relationship? Perhaps they want the security of a relationship but see the responsibility more as an encumbrance on the way that they want to live their lives. Should this attitude shelter their actions toward others? Why? Why, should this form of mentality exist at all?

At every moment in our lives, we have the opportunity to treat others with respect. At some point in the relationship you have to face the fact that even if you truly love someone, they may refuse to see that you want and need to be loved also. Even when they are treated with respect, they fail to feel the importance of this critical emotion. It is like the sound of a silent rain to those who refuse to listen.

Face to face they say all of the right things that give you hope, and allow you to hang on from day-to-day. Then suddenly they walk away with no apparent memory of what they said, or the responsibility they carry in the relationship.

In a perfect world, it should be easier for one person to find that special mate to share their dream life with. But this is an imperfect world, and mankind itself is not a perfect species. Cold Love has caused our beliefs, and knowledge of what True Love is to become so obscured, making it almost impossible to obtain. Our need for instant gratification is pushing mankind toward an oblivious realm of existence.

Some may rationalize that we have been subjected to Cold Love for such an extended period of time that we have come to believe that this is the only form of love to be known. Nonsense! True Love does still exist. We could not know real love if we had not had the experience of Cold Love to guide our interpretation. How could one judge truth, if lies are all that was heard? How could one sense the truth in a person's soul, if deceit was only known? Most of us have journeyed to both sides, and the truth is that it does not have to be this way. There are other ways to live out our lives and to express love. It is merely a choice we alone make.

Perhaps we have played the role of victim and transgressor within our lifetime. If during those times we could not see the truth that these roles offer, then we are failing in our attempt to evolve mentally. Our dreams will become clouded in unwanted visions. If this continues, we may live out our entire life merely wandering day-to-day, not finding our true path.

There are responsibilities in any type of relationship that must be understood. Responsibilities include caring enough about your mate to allow them to grow as a person and allow them to grow with you or you with them. Two people must first care for themselves, and then for the relationship. If a person feels self-worth, without being self-riotous, then they will give more of themselves to the relationship. They do not fear the relationship. They know in their hearts that their love is strong, and they are with each other in spirit. They would give up, or live their life for each other. That's true love.

Part of the communication process in relationships is the demand for an open and honest exchange of beliefs and feelings. Communication is the number one key that couples of long-term relationships will disclose as their secret. They have conquered their innermost fears and will allow openness and deep loving emotions to guide their lives. They have found a secret to longevity in love and in most cases a longer happier life.

Some may feel that their lives have been out of control for so long that they present barriers in a relationship as a form of protection. They may never free their hearts to open and honest love. They carry the mental scars that present themselves as what some may interpret as hostile. They do not communicate well and present a very aggressive nature when a thing doesn't go just right. They feel that they must have greater control over their lives, or they may feel to be lost forever. Their thoughts and actions are the epitome of Cold Love. A greater understanding of the affects that Cold Love presents within our everyday lives may allow you to gain a higher degree of control over the effects.

Chapter 18 - The White Knight Syndrome

The *White Knight Syndrome* may often be described as an overwhelming urge to give your emotions, or caring, to someone that is hurting from a bad relationship or to someone that just wants a person close so they don't feel so alone and vulnerable. In those moments of decision to get involved, we may think we know what caused the failed relationship's issues, or that we know the person we are trying to help. But in reality, we likely do not. We are at times bias and favor one person's side over the other, which is a natural thing to do. There are always at least two sides to every relationship story, and the majority of the relevant facts may never be known to you or anyone else outside of the personal involvement. Perhaps we are attracted to that person we see as in need, and we take advantage of the situation by offer our caring in hopes of obtaining a connection. Many rationalize that this is not a selfish intent, yet it often turns out to be the case.

Perhaps you knew their partner as well, seeing the relationship degrade over time, and you witnessed the neglectful or abusive interactions. This is a very common trap that many fall victims to, but trying to rescue someone in, or from, a bad relationship is not a good idea or the long-term answer to their situation.

Regardless if you knew the person previously or not, if this person wants out of a bad relationship then it's their responsibility alone to remove themselves from it. If they choose to rebound into a relationship with you, they are being irresponsible to say the least. They are taking the seemingly quick and easy route as they immerse you into their own personal problems. Problems that were not of your making, but you will now have to deal with them as your intimate support is offered. Being sympathetic or compassionate toward others is a noble thing to do, but this form of caring can be presented in other ways and with far less risk to everyone involved.

It may feel very natural for you to want to jump in and help this person you have feelings for, but it's their responsibility alone to deal with what caused the breakup and the aftermath. Only then, once they have healed, not under the influence of the offending past relationship, can they be free to choose another without selfish intent. How can you know for certain if this person truly cares for you in the ways you desire? Are they within the proper mental state to be seeking a long-term relationship, or will your caring be only a means to their end goal?

Putting yourself in the middle of a potentially dangerous situation such as a break-up is not the smartest thing we could do, nor is this effort likely to be successful. You could find yourself being attacked from both sides if they decide to reconcile, or physically harmed in the defense of the person you are trying to defend and protect. Nothing enrages an ex-boyfriend or ex-girlfriend as much as seeing their departed mate with someone else so soon after a breakup. You will appear to have been involved with their ex-mate before the break-up occurred and perhaps the person that cause it.

The real truth of the matter is, we do not wholeheartedly understand the situations that caused the problems that the other person is going through. We are an outsider, likely accepting a one-sided viewpoint. All we may feel is an attraction or caring, so we are willing to take greater risks. In these times, we appear to be so eager to paint that proverbial target on our backs then run through the firing range of life. By taking such great risk, we may inadvertently be positioning ourselves to be hurt. It may be true that the other person is going through a bad relationship, and you could help in many ways, but you should try to be a friend first and support them with some degree of distance. Putting yourself between two people going through these types of situations can and often does get out of hand until someone is seriously injured.

If we decide to get more intimately attached, and before you realize what has happened, you may find yourself involved in a relationship that is not ready for you, and you are not prepared for all the drama or conflict it may bring. Within that past relationship of the person you desire to help, even if physical abuse was not an issue, there may still have been a lot of mental wounds that require time to heal. Are you to be this person's rescuer and White Knight, or just their temporary band-aid until they have what they need from you? If we step into this type of broken relationship too soon, we must mentally accept the fact that this may all blow-up in our face soon. Once that happens, then we have our own broken relationship to deal with, and it is likely that no one will come to our rescue.

Weight out the facts mentioned earlier. If someone has suffered in a Cold Love relationship, they may not currently be their true selves. It may take some time before this person will recover and for their true personality to present itself again. Some may recover completely over time while others manage only to a marginal degree, depending upon the severity and damage presented. Try to maintain some distance until the other relationship is dissolved entirely. Give them some time to deal with their problems in their own way and allow them the period needed to heal. After some time passing, if there is enough common ground for you both to build a meaningful relationship, then there exist a much better chance of the connection becoming long-lasting. If they don't want to wait and they soon steer their lives in other directions, you must believe that it is for the best. Stop and examine the reasons why you want to be close to this person. Are you doing what is right for you? Is this "White Night Syndrome" so strong that you cannot see the danger that is present?

Perhaps you are also involved in a bad relationship, so there is a common ground to be shared. Talking becomes so easy for both of you. Swapping war-stories, so to speak, is a form of understanding of your situation so you relate to them effortlessly. At last, someone that understands what you are going through. It may be helpful if we can understand or remember that distress is the calling card of grief and torment needs an ear to validate its pain. And most importantly; "Fools rush in where wise men fear to tread".

It doesn't matter what situation ignites the White Night Syndrome. That which is more important is that we realize and understand what emotions are taking place with each person involved. Who are we truly trying to rescue here? What do we hope to accomplish in the long run? Often, we get so engulfed in our own loses, or loneliness, that we become blinded to our true motives.

Perhaps we are searching so hard to find our happiness that we forget that "happiness" is not a place, it's a state of mind. Why would you want to fill your metaphoric half-empty glass with someone else's relationship problems? You may also inadvertently stifle their ability to see what is best for them. Misery may love company, but misery also feeds on misery. Be a good friend and share your insights into what you have learned about Cold Love with them, then let them decide.

The White Knight Syndrome is not specific to the male gender who is often viewed as the guy who wants to rush-in and rescue the so-called "damsel in distress". Women can exhibit these characteristics just as easily. We are often taught during early childhood that women are the primary emotional caretakers in a relationship, although this has become debatable in modern times. Numerous studies have shown that females can and do exhibit these White Knight traits, though it may present itself in different ways than males.

What does the "White Knight Syndrome" have to do with "Cold Love" you may ask? Well, perhaps not all-encompassing, but for many people, they are idealizing the other person, perhaps putting them on a pedestal, and taking the concept of chivalry a bit beyond it's intended meaning. The male may be actively drawn to women, or vice-versa, who appears to be helpless and of needing to be supported. In some case studies, it was determined that some may treat the other person's needs as extensions of their own. While some may use criticisms and numerous forms of patronizing to undermine the mental states of the other. These are forms of controlling others under the guise of "just trying to help." Talk about a slippery slope!

The aspects of "Cold Love" may be viewed most clearly when the resentment starts to occur. Resentment towards the seemingly rescued person who does not return their undying love and loyalty. This often occurs because the rescuer was not necessarily acting out of pure kindness but with the expectation that their own selfish needs would be fulfilled and that they would be rewarded for their efforts. This mindset of *"quid-pro-quo"* most often only works when both participating parties are in agreement to the expected results or exchange upfront.

Rescuing someone is a noble thing to do, but we must understand that the characteristics of Cold Love may be so overwhelming to the point that the sympathy presented towards others can quickly revert to a high state of self-denial, allowing us to forget that our partner is solely responsible for their behavior. Sympathetic to the point where you are more prone to making excuses for them, believing that they "can't help themselves", so you then become an enabler helping to hide their destructive behavior, trying to shield them from the consequences of their actions or accountability. You may at first have been viewed as their White Knight, but you may quickly become so codependent that now you need to be rescued. Feeling compassion for others is a gallant thing to do, but without boundaries to the extent of harming yourself is very destructive.

Chapter 19 - The Burning Hatred Inside

The victims of Cold Love relationships often describe a lingering burning hatred inside, at times felt both for themselves and the other person involved. What many people fail to see initially is what this form of inner-hatred can do to their overall mental health. Hatred can be described simplistically as a reversed loving passion. Something once held as special to you has turned dark and ugly, more powerful than you can seemingly control at times. Such hurt and anguish can build to a level that it may take over what is left of a person's heart. Memories of the way you were before you were hurt seem so distant. At present, hatred and anger have consumed you.

In your thoughts, go back to a time before, try to remember a specific event before you were hurt, when you enjoyed the good times before this past relationship turned bad. Attempt to resolve how you got involved with this person that has hurt you, recalling the events in detail if possible. Consider the things that created the attraction, see them from that different perspective, if only for this moment. Try to resolve how you allowed someone to connect with you so intimately, then allowed to treat you in such ways that have brought you so much pain.

How many times in your life have you heard someone tell another, or maybe someone has told you, that the best way to get over a failed relationship is to find someone else? True that we may rationalize that we will move slow and try to be more careful this time. Are those old, and maybe not so wise-tales, impairing our judgment? Is this truly the right thing to do? In what manner will you approach this goal? Do we truly believe that any person can find that "Mr. or Miss Right" with all of the torment from a recent breakup boiling up inside them? How could anyone feel pure love when rage dominates their thoughts and stands as an ominous barrier?

In our everyday life, we give off mental signals or cues that many others can sense. Our every thought resonates and speaks of who and what we are at that moment. If we allow hatred to dwell within us, with all of the distress it brings, what type of persons are we most likely to attract?

What about the way you carry on with your life? Are you the best that you can be at work, or at just being yourself? You try to concentrate on what is important in your life, but memories appear as a dark phantom in your thoughts. We must remember that we still have to care about ourselves first. We have to find the light at the end of the tunnel within our essence. If we can't care about the person we are, how could we be allowed to find someone to care for us respectfully and properly?

Why should we allow hate? Hate is a burning passion, geared toward self-destruction. Who are we trying to punish? If you want to stop hurting, then you must first forgive yourself. Soon after, the memories of your loss will fade. Find a reason to be good to yourself, if just for this moment, then perhaps for a day. Even the deepest cut will heal if given proper care and time.

If you are trying to get over someone, try spending some time alone with your thoughts. Look around and see the positives in your life. Being alone is so important at this time. Solitude can offer the opportunity for you to deal with your inner hurt without interference from other influences. Getting advice from a friend may ease your pain momentarily but others can't heal your pain long-term.

Still, your gut hurts! So much anger and frustration have taken a deep-seated hold on your heart. Some will confess that the deeper a person had loved someone, the more intensely they felt hatred toward them. See how things can turn? Perhaps we can learn to not give ourselves entirely until we find that special someone who is deserving. A person who would give their life if it meant saving yours. There are those out there that feel this way about the people they love, we just need to find them.

There may come a time in any relationship when a person tries to hang on to a love for someone, but deep inside they know their partner does not truly love them in return. It is such a hard thing to admit. Echoes of "why can't they love me in return" haunts our innermost thoughts.

What is it that prevents me from being happy, you may ask? You have given all that you have, physically and mentally. At times you felt as if you were lying to yourself. Hoping that you will not lose this life that you have grown so accustomed to. You start to think that you just can't stay any longer, you feel so saddened. Your inner voice speaks that you are more deserving. Perhaps deep in your heart, you knew your current situation would not last. The warning signs were there but you chose to ignore them.

During your contemplation, you must understand that Hate is purely an emotional state, not a life sentence of condemnation. If allowed, hatred will invoke feelings of *animosity*, anger, or resentment toward not only the person or individual who harmed you, it will infest your perceptions of reality. Things that once made you happy may no longer find a place in your heart. You could find yourself turning away from the friends you once cared for, as you now question all that you once believed in. Some studies show that when we hate intensely, we often allow our mistrust to consume us, to govern our lives. We give-up control to an emotion that offers only negatives.

Many have asked; "Can you hate someone you once truly loved?", which is a difficult question to answer because that answer is not always so black or white. On the surface, we would consider that we definitely can develop hatred toward that person. Psychologically speaking, digging deeper into the issue, we may then conclude that both love and hate are similar, as they are an emotional reaction to a person whom we became emotionally dependent upon for numerous reasons we may not have cognizant reasoning to explain. What if we could conclude that we don't actually hate the person? What if, we just hate the situation they have created and we are focusing our despair onto that person as hatred?

What often happens within our romantic connections when we at first fall in love with someone is that we desire the complete acceptance of our love and affection. Once this happens, we then seek the perfection of having that same degree of love returned to us. However, if that person fails to reciprocate, or return that love sufficiently, our minds will view this as a one-sided relationship and that initiates our feelings of disappointment.

Why is it that a person's hate is felt and handled differently when you compare a romantic relationship to other relationship types? Consider the relationship you have with your siblings, parents or other close family members. Surely these people have disappointed you in some way, at times appearing to not love you as much as you feel love for them. This is due to the basic family-love bond. When this bond is damaged, you may feel hurt, excluded or even angry, but that family-love bond remains, allowing forgiveness to find its place. This may present further evidence that we don't truly hate the person, though we do hate the fact we are not getting the full consideration we feel we deserve. Within the family setting, compromise is much easier, even when no one appears to want to give up anything. We seem to have the ability to step-back and cool-off quicker with our close family.

When we evaluate "The Burning Hatred Inside" it must be understood that this form of emotional invasion alters our inner state of being to a degree that it changes our thought structure. Within this state of mind, a person is subjected to a higher risk of errors in their cognitive abilities. Their thoughts are distorted and have a major impact on how the individual interprets what is happening around them. This felt hate causes a person to be angry as their interpretations become egocentric, and they will often exaggerate the frequency of the adverse events in their lives thus further exacerbating the underlying problem.

Our minds are programmed to interpret what happens to us by our belief structure and our preconceptions from that we have obtained from previous experiences, our self-conditioning. Even if we attempt to hide our hate-filled thoughts, they are there, influencing our subconscious mind. Seeming dormant, yet still allowed to shape our behavior and values in life. Having these damaging influences causing dysfunctional beliefs will always influence what aspects of a situation we focus on, how we interpret that experience, and how we respond to it.

Hatred is a devaluation of one's self if it is allowed to persist. Hatred can invoke extreme violent reactive behaviors causing further damage in an endless cycle. Hatred is a fuel to Cold Love, feeding off of each other, expanding with alike intensity, exaggerating our misinterpretations.

Clinical observations have shown that hate can be controlled. When people learn to focus their attention on their automatic thoughts, to look beyond the hurt with a critical eye, intentionally replacing negative thoughts with that which is more realistic, more kind. Through this exercise, people feel less angry, less intense, and recover from negative stimuli more quickly.

Chapter 20 - Question Yourself

Perhaps certain questions can never be asked within an already questionable relationship, and certainly there exist many questions that should be asked. But the questions that will benefit us most, are the ones that we ask and answer sincerely to ourselves. After all, these efforts are to help ourselves primarily, as we can't hope to direct change onto others. Not being one-hundred percent honest with your mate is one issue, but being honest with yourself is paramount. If we spend our lives avoiding our inner truth, how will we ever become a whole person? Who is the real you? What do you truly want in this life, and what measures are you willing to take to achieve your success or happiness?

We must find the inner strength to allow our true-self to come forward. Talk to your inner self! You can be a far better friend to yourself than anyone else could ever imagine being. Have you ever noticed that at times we treat our friends better than we treat ourselves? If you suffocate your true beliefs and feelings, perhaps to go-along or get-along, then ask yourself "why". Why is it that another person's opinion of me is more important than the way I feel about myself? Are you allowing others to set your self-worth? If so, how does one measure themselves against another? Against a person, or persons, who are so different than we are, or have a background that may not be so similar to our own? In most cases, no two people are precisely alike, nor do they feel or react to stimuli in the same manner. Every person that has ever existed upon this earth is different, to at least some degree, many to a large degree. Are you so willing to be what others want you to be and to give up on your individuality? Are you aware that others will value you more if they know you are an honest and kind person, a loving and compassionate person, and above all an individual mind?

How can you be honest with others if you are not true to yourself?

Has your current relationship pushed you to the point that you think; "Why should I consider the other person's feelings when they do not appear to care about mine?". Of course, you deserve all of the respect in-turn that you show for others. Ask yourself; "Why am I allowing another person to treat me disrespectfully when I am undeserving of their wrath?". Some people give and give of themselves until nothing is left to keep themselves happy. If you have surrounded yourself with people who only take from you, what's left, who will support you in your time of need?

In the past, if after entering into a relationship, perhaps days or months later, did you notice a distance begin to build? Do you at times detect those little pot-shots, that jab that was taken at you, for no apparent reason? Some may try to write this off jokingly, but in reality, it is a form of passive-aggressive behavior that can and often does hurt you or others. Why must you adsorb this form of treatment and ponder on for days inwardly doubting your true worth, your true emotions? If you were with the right person, they would allow you to feel your worth. They would never attempt to cause hurt or harm to you.

When your state of mind is doubtful, do you often consider the difference between what you truly love and what you think you need? Loving someone because you need them, or because you fear to be alone may still be a sort of love, but you also need to realize that these are characteristics and indicators of Cold Love. No one should feel as if they need someone else to feel whole as a person. Reflect on both who you are now and who you truly want to be. If you are unhappy with your life then only you can change that, only you can make your life better, fuller and more enriched.

Yes! Question yourself! Don't fear your doubt, embrace it. Even if you are afraid, that same fear is meant to guide you, protect you, not to debilitate. Doubt is often seeded by negative feedback or bad experiences. But these same experiences should allow you to see what doesn't work for you as a person, and just as important what does. Resolve the doubt in your mind. Seek out what is best for you and learn to know what is right. Once known, you then have that knowledge, and with knowledge comes the gift of wisdom. Wisdom contains the understanding and offers both intelligence and forgiveness, allowing change to occur. No need to punish yourself for what went wrong, just don't continue making the same mistakes. You will become a stronger, more loving and a better person for it. People spend their entire life trying to be like someone else. They will never know what gifts they could have brought to this world. What a waste of a lifetime.

As far back as the mid-seventeenth century, Descartes described the art of "to think about thinking itself", and coined the phrase; "I think, therefore I am". Descartes theorized that we must abandon our thoughts about anything that can be doubted because that thing, whatever it is, is fundamentally uncertain. As participants in life, do we not owe it to ourselves to doubt that which troubles us or makes us feel uncertain about our wellbeing? And, for centuries to follow now, many have come to understand that it is our very ability to doubt and to think intelligently that makes us *sentient* beings.

Questioning yourself should not be debilitating, it should be enlightening. As we question our old beliefs or interactions, in a forthright manner, we may see things in a new and different way, a way that helps us to grow as an individual. If we can question the past and learn from our mistakes, then our future life and relationships stand a much better chance of being successful.

Have you ever thought or said; "if I could only turn back time and change what happened?". Wouldn't that be wonderful if we could? Unfortunately, the ability to travel through time is not an option presently, nor will it be within the foreseeable future, if ever. Instead, what if we question all that is not right in our life now, and start working to make the changes necessary to prevent additional and similar negative occurrences in the future? What if, years from now, we find ourselves living that happy life, being in love, having the loving family, not doubting our self-worth, all because we put in the required effort now to make that brighter future? This is possible, and highly probable if we can only believe in ourselves.

Question yourself and your life choices. Make a list of things you want or need to change. If those changes are possible to make and plausible, then why not proceed. What do you have to lose other than a lot of unhappiness and self-doubt? Don't plan or expect everything on your list to change overnight or you may become disheartened and give up quickly. Make the changes in small steps, then build on each success. Jokingly said was the riddle; "How do you eat an elephant? Answer - One bite at a time!" Even if it takes months or years to reach your overall goal, it's still better than being unhappy for the rest of your life.

To some degree, a person must teach themselves how to be happy, removing as many negatives from their lives as possible. It also stands to reason that the earlier in life we learn these positive lessons the longer our happiness can be lived. Just the act of questioning ourselves is a good first step toward learning how to make our life better. If we truly want happiness to fill our life, then we have to teach our minds how to achieve it.

Within the early mid-twentieth century, a behavioral psychologist concluded that; "a behavior that evokes a pleasurable response is more likely to be repeated than behavior that evokes an unpleasant one. In short, find the pleasurable things in your life. Making the same mentally unhealthy choices over and over again expecting a different result is the definition of insanity. Once you start removing the negatives in your life, find the positives. Fill your life with the happiness that you deserve.

Chapter 21 - Cold Love's Fallout

All around the world millions of people are playing a part in Cold Love relationships, most without realizing. Be it a marriage, friendship, or just everyday social interactions. Not only are they not aware of the mental forces guiding them, their friends and families can't understand why anyone would choose the dark path they have taken. Millions of situations where the proper form of love, the warm sincere type of love, is not being exchanged. Cold Love can infect any form of relationship if allowed. No one person is immune.

Cold Love is not a present-day mental infestation. Cold Love has existed throughout time, evolving with humanity, ever-changing in its efforts to elude detection. Cold Love is like a virus, affecting its carrier making them a victim, and can be spread by the daily interaction with others. Cold Love is often passed on to one's children, family, and many others. Cold Love is not considered to be genetically hereditary, although it is something that can be passed on by what is considered to be a form of environmental heredity.

How we treat others, or what we teach and expose our children to, are often things that many rationalize as normal, no matter how abnormal the actions may be to some. Similar to a child watching their parents argue for years, the child matures thinking that this form of interaction is normal in a relationship. The parent's interactions create stimuli to all witnessing. Stimuli that is similar to programming computer. This learned behavior can cause our children to seek-out similar interactions within their adulthood relationships, or seek what is most familiar to them.

Consider "cause & effect". The "cause" manifest because of the way many of us live our lives. Perhaps in fear of what they don't understand, they allow themselves to participate in hate-filled actions, or accepting the lies that exist within their relationships without taking action to prevent or cure the issue. The "effect" can be seen as the emotional consequence often displayed within our overall manner of living.

A factor that we must bring to light is our children. The children of hundreds of generations have grown with examples of Cold Love being paraded before them in abundance. Try to tell a child, "do as I say, not as I do," and you are a fool to think that the child will conform to your will. Children will most often mimic and accept their environment as being normal. All forms of stimuli presented to a child from those who have influenced their lives have presented mental programmed in some degree.

In the early 1900s, Social Psychologists at Yale University experimented on just how far a person's environmental conditions can go in shaping behavior and beliefs. Findings were that within a family setting, children will most often take on the persona of that person they see as "in power", or even of someone without authority over them if the exposure is prevalent.

Numerous studies also showed that even the most seemingly psychologically healthy people can act-out with extreme cruelty, if misguided. This is not to infer that Cold Love is necessarily cruel or extreme in its entirety, but it does show that the many forms of Cold Love will be accepted as correct by those exposed to it for extended durations, or if it is the only exposure available to mold a young mind.

Children have grown up in certain environments where the meaning of true love was tremendously skewed. As they mature into adulthood and seek-out their true love, they present or find what fits into their understanding of what love is supposed to be. How could they do more, unless taught otherwise? The meaning of true love was never presented in their innermost programming. Their environmental conditioning has taught them that physical violence or mentally hurting another person is acceptable, their known examples. They have witnessed that cheating and lying within even the closest of relationships is acceptable, so this is now viewed as a normal part of life. It is difficult for a person who has grown up in certain environments to know of any other way. They cannot find the real or true love that they seek as it was never present in their past.

Another area of psychological study that evaluates the effects of stimuli on humans is called; "Desensitization", or "Conditioning". Ivan Pavlov pioneered these studies back in the late 1800s, followed by Joseph Wolpe's expanded works which occurred well into the 20th Century. However, the bulk of the research performed and the application of "desensitization techniques" have mostly been focused on treatment to overcome issues relating to abnormal psychological issues like phobias and other anxiety disorders. From many perspectives, their use of this technique was to treat the outcome or the result of the previous exposure to negative mental conditioning. Within this effort to better understand the fall-out of what Cold Love may present in our everyday lives, we want to address the cause of such negative actions. If we can better recognize the traits of what Cold Love exhibits, then we have a better chance to counter its effects. Why wait until the damage has occurred if we can take preventative measures?

Perhaps some children never had the exposure to the proper kind of love that they needed, so they often turn to the camaraderie of other influencers such as cults or street gangs, or they jump at the first opportunity they have to get away from their current not-so-good situation or the authority of the family setting. All of the intimacy and fellowship that they seek are there, drawing them in, at first at least.

The search for the true meaning of love and trust has become a Judas in our society. It may have all started with a single lie or an occurrence of someone being cruel to another. A single person not wanting to face the responsibility of their misdeeds could damage many generations to come if these understandings are not corrected.

Another form, or fall-out, of Cold Love, is the person that you have become. Consider all that seems right to us that others find puzzling. Have you ever called someone a, "self-righteous so and so"? All you are saying is that the other person thinks that they are right all the time. However, you may be ignoring the fact that from their perspective they feel righteous. Are we so pure, so firmly planted within our version of what is right that we judge others so harshly? Are we so close-minded in our understanding and beliefs?

Consider this. Has any form of Cold Love implanted itself into your understanding? When and how did it happen? Is this something that you could pass-on to a child or a partner unwillingly?

If we were exposed to these forms of cold-heartiness, then those many traits may be seeded into our understanding of what love is supposed to be. Can our interpretations be anything more than what we have been conditioned to believe? As our minds develop through the years, we store information as an interpretation. Exposure to negative influences, even for a short period of time, can greatly influence our understanding.

Our relationship partners, our friends, and family may have a greater impact on our lives than we first consider, even more so than our formal teachers. Our attention may be greater directed to those that we consider loves or cares for us the most. How is it that we make determinations of what is more correct, or who is directing us onto the right path? Not all partners, friends, family, nor teachers have all of the correct answers. What we believe to be true is all that we consider at the time of contemplation. Hopefully, through our interpretation of the situations presented we try to weed out what is more correct, but that's not always easy to do.

During your teen years in school, you encountered all types of attitudes in your association with other children. Perhaps their influence on you is not always so evident. Think about all of the peer pressure that you have been subjected to. When others taunted you, how did that make you feel? If you failed a test, how low did your self-esteem sink? Cold Love is not always apparent. There may have been many situations in your life that were out of line, cruel, and handled the wrong way, but what did this do to you deep inside?

Think of a situation from a past relationship that still haunts you. Ask yourself that if at that time that person had been more kind and loving to you, would this have allowed or encouraged you to be a more considerate and understanding person in your present relationships or everyday life?

Yes, Cold Love has fall-out and leaves its mental scares behind for us to deal with. Cold Love presents little-to-no joy or peace of mind. It allows little-to-no fellowship with others or satisfaction with the things that should make you happy. Cold Love causes anger, disappointment, bitterness, and robes us of our self-worth. Cold Love can cause a person to coldheartedly walk away from their responsibilities, their marriage, their children, the obligations to their work or to society overall. Cold Love can dissolve the conscience mind allowing no morality to exist. Cold Love can also cause a person to become extremely self-centered, arrogant, greedy, defiant and rebellious. Knowing the cause of these issues allows an opportunity to challenge the encounter early on.

Chapter 22 - Seeking Our Heaven on Earth

How many of us are wondering if there will come a day when we can look into another's eyes and feel true love again? Or, can we find that special person that allows us to feel blessed as we feel their warm presence even when they are far away?

Listen intently as you contemplate or speak-out of the things that you sincerely love. Listen to that inner voice that we often push aside or mask. Perhaps your "Heaven on Earth" is not an eternity away. Perhaps it is just before you waiting for you to find it, or to earn the rewards. To find that someone that cares for the real you, and could answer all of your hopes and end this solitude of the heart. You may think that this special someone may already belong to another, but how could you know that to be certain. Perhaps they are thinking the same as you, out there somewhere searching for someone just like you. Take a chance on happiness. The rewards far outweigh the risk you must take.

Imagine meeting that person for the first time, and a connection is made. The conversation flows like a surging river, such as the love in your heart that wants to be free and giving. It seems as if you have so much in common as if you had known each other for years even though you have never met previously. The hurt and mistrust from the past may be present inside you, and that fear of not knowing if you could ever find the right person to be a part of your life still dwells, but you have to keep trying. Otherwise, you accept failure which ends all hope.

Every person must learn from their past, or continue to make the same mistakes presenting the same consequences. Was there a past relationship that you entered into quickly, without a true connection felt, only to see it deteriorate and fail? Examine your past loves and relationships. How many times before did you enter into a relationship only to soon feel that you were not with the right person? Why do we spend most of our life trying to convince ourselves that we have all that we deserve? Are we so complacent within our wants and needs in this life? Can we see that brighter hope shining through that is trying to show us the way?

Millions of us, every day, settle for less than what we want. Then soon after a bitterness for life starts to build inside us like a toxic infestation, eating away at our true-selves until we no longer feel alive. Why do we hesitate so long in paying the price required to find true love? Are we simply making choices that merely pacify our immediate needs, for days or weeks, then soon months or years passing? Our spirit wants to reach out and find what we desire but we hesitate out of fear.

You may often feel that you must speak out, especially if you're not certain if this person is right for you. You may be fearful that you will drive them away, but you have to make your intentions clear and reveal what you truly want in the relationship. There may be times when you feel as though your lonely heart is in control, often winning over your exhausted inner judgments. It is within these times that you have to find the strength to push forward. Take that chance to unveil your innermost desires. If your mate is right for you, they will understand and become more open and abiding with you. We have to find this open communication if we want our relationship to survive.

If you do not come forward in this manner, perhaps this is not your way. Perhaps you choose to take an easier route, accepting only what others offer. If so, then you must accept that there is always a price to pay for not being true to yourself. For some of us, we know that if we do not speak our heart's intent, we will feel regret later on for not doing so.

True that if we speak out honestly, we may scare-off a potential mate. But, if by you expressing your inner truth this doesn't bring you closer to them, then perhaps they can't appreciate your true intentions, which is a warning sign. Speaking your truth may be viewed as an intrusion to them, as they may not be agreeable in giving you all that you deserve. After knowing your desires, they may view this as an intrusion into their version of what they want you to see as the truth. They may feel crowded, unsure of how to handle your clearly stated emotions. Try to keep in mind that open communications should be good for both partners, if the relationship has any real ground to build on.

If you play the so-called games that couples often play with and against each other, then you are masking your true desires, which will haunt your innermost wishes. Each may gain some form of short-term gratification, but in the long run both are being misled and precious moments are lost. If something becomes of this new mislead relationship and you start spending a lot of time with this person, you may soon find yourself with a stranger, and feeling very lonely inside.

We all must find the strength to be ourselves, to speak our minds, be that unique person that only we can be. If you say something that the other person takes out of context or something that makes them withdraw, then you have screened them out. Move on and know that you can't settle for less than what you desire, regardless of how hard you try. Short-term gratification may appear to be better than being alone, but is the hurt worth it in the long-run?

The many forms of "game-playing" are accountable for the extraordinary divorce rate now assaulting this world.

Consider who is the blame for this. In many cases, this is also the reason for the violence that develops in relationships. We soon realize that we have invested in something that we do not want or believe in. Our disappointments can, and often does, turn inward and develop into anger.

By playing these games, you not only fooled another person, you also fooled yourself. Eventually, this mental game-playing becomes an annoyance, then perhaps evolves into anger against ourselves. Initially, we feel the brunt of this camouflaging of desires, but will soon find that we are taking out our frustrations on others. Couples will pull further and further apart as they try to regain their true selves. Even in a divorcing situation, we are playing a destructive game if we have convinced ourselves that we must hate this person to pull away from them. Most view hate as an emotion expressed outwardly, but they fail to realize that hate begins within. Hate that may consume everything that once made you a good person.

If we ever hope to find our "Heaven on Earth", perhaps we must first pay-the-price for that blessing. Finding true love is not a simple gift to be given, it must be earned. This atonement is possible and can happen if we heighten our understanding of what Cold Love is and how it has infested our daily lives. Only then can we determine the methods required to change Cold Love's effects. Once understood, then assert ways to shield ourselves from it.

Chapter 23 - Risk and Reward

Should it be that we must choose not to love at all? Is this to be our only sanction against heartbreak, against Cold Love? Does true love exist for us? If so, where does it dwell? What measure must we take to find our true path to happiness?

Why is it that we are so willing to enter into a situation with someone even when we are uncertain of the outcome? To risk so much, even when we know that the possibility of finding that Mr. or Ms. Right is similar to winning a Lottery? Our past has shown us that the odds are not in our favor, yet we continue to risk it all. Perhaps it's because we know that if we don't take these risks then we can never win the prize?

Is it the unpredictability of the situation that lures us in? It seems that no matter how bad our past relationships may have been, we still maintain that glimmer of hope that the next relationship effort will be better. This, of course, should be true, but it is also what makes us vulnerable at times if we continue evaluating our perceptions and interactions as we always have.

During some of the most horrific of relationships, perhaps in an attempt to rationalize our decisions or efforts, we often tell ourselves that; "everything happens for a reason". Really? Is that true or merely an attempt to allow justification for the harm we either caused or allowed? It may be truer that there is a "reason for everything that happens", as defined by *The Laws of Cause and Effect*.

To allow ourselves to conclude that harmful life events were purposely set into motion by some outside omnipotent force just to teach us a life-lesson is unreasonable and could suggest that a form of paranoia is greatly influencing our judgments. Is it so hard to admit that we are not a perfect species? Is this suggestion of being paranoid offensive to you? If so, dealing with the effects of Cold Love will be a long and treacherous road for you. Understand the problem and deal with it.

To some degree, we are all paranoid in some manner. We all are at times suspicious of other's motives, believing that others want to harm us without just cause. We may be reluctance to confide in others, seldom open to express our dislikes, often finding demeaning or threatening insinuations in even the most innocent of comments or events, and are at times easy to anger or feel hostility toward others. Admitting that we may have a problem is a good positive step toward resolving our issues. Most often, a person with a paranoid personality doesn't believe that their behavior is abnormal. It may seem completely rational for them to be overly suspicious of others. Seeking advice from a professional is an option, yet not always necessary. This is something you can concur on your own if you so choose.

We have to understand that even if things do not turn out as we had hoped, we should have at least learned some sort of positive lesson from the experiences. Did we? Will we take that new knowledge and do our best to not make the same mistakes again? If so, and by truly understanding ourselves better and having the will to change our perceptions, we can then reap more rewards and take less risk.

Even notice that when we first meet someone that we find ourselves agreeing with most of their opinions? Listening to all of their stories so intently? Laughing at even their half-witted jokes? Going to places where you are not truly comfortable? Being around their friends when you do not feel that they want to be close to you? Is it because of our wanting so much to find love and be in a solid relationship that we tend to skew our judgment and our level of feelings toward others? Is this being paranoid, or just the reality of the situations?

Then only after a few dates, as the weeks pass, your gut starts to tell you that you could never love this person, or you don't feel real love or compassion from them as you should. You may be asking yourself; "What happened". You are trying so hard, giving everything that you know how to give, freely sharing intimate relations with them, but still, the warmth is not there, you feel no spark or true connection. Now, even the way they touch you feels cold and distant, more of a predetermined task required to reach their ultimate objective, and with no sincerity. You start to notice a change in their attitude toward you, and their change is changing your version of you. Your initial vision of them as a person appears to be dwindling away and destroying the entire relationship effort. You want more in a relationship, more of a connection, and now the fear of starting over rears-up its ugly head, infecting your thoughts constantly. For the risk taken, little reward seems achievable.

There are many reasons why we do some of the things that we do, and the right decision by one person may not be the right decision for another. Each of us is so different in so many ways. We each choose from a varied list of options that are before us each day. Why is it that some seem to always make the right chose, and others are constantly pit-falling every time they turn around? One thing for certain is, what works for one couple, or another relationship, may not contain the secrets to our success. No matter how long it takes, or how hard the journey, we must find what works for us.

Taking chances is just a part of life itself. On each day we are lucky enough to wake from our beds, we immediately start taking chances, even if we are just taking out the trash or within our commute to work, we are taking chances. There does not exist now, nor will ever exist a person on this earth who can offer a 100% guarantee that they will be alive tomorrow or even a few hours from now. That's a hard fact that no one can ignore.

We can't shelter ourselves totally from the many ways to be mentally hurt or physically injured, or prevent death when your time comes. Nor can we totally shelter ourselves from getting hunt within a relationship, or for being used to satisfy someone else's desires all without an ounce of remorse. So! Here is the problem! Through electrochemical analysis, research determined long ago that the human species, every man, woman, and child, carries a different level of cognizant ability to feel different forms of emotions. Great effort has taken place to better understand why people act and feel the way they do. Studies were meticulously performed to better understand how some people can inflict great atrocities onto others, inflicting horrible circumstances on others, and why they do so, totally without remorse. These results help to confirm what levels of intensity a specific person may feel about a specific condition, situation, or action, and why others feel very differently.

If you haven't found your true love up to this point, then you will have to continue taking those chances. The best we can hope for is that it's different the next time and that happiness doesn't elude us once more. If we arm ourselves with a new or different level of understanding, our chances improve.

The many statements within this book's writing are not always warm and easy to hear, but they are necessary. If one can come to understand what Cold Love is and how it can affect our everyday lives, especially our relationships, then we are better equipped to deal with issues on a day-to-day basis. Believe in yourself, and allow these teachings to make you a better friend, lover, and life-partner. It can all be viewed as our attitude toward life itself.

Our attitude can present a psychological phenomenon, reflecting our knowledgeable insights, positive experiences, our likes or desires, and an expression of the way we choose to live our lives. Our attitude is formed through a process of self-evaluation influenced by various factors such as perceptive reasoning, positive actions, and inspirational behavior. We are who we allow ourselves to be. Take the risk to make yourself a better person and the rewards will come to you.

Chapter 24 - The Foundations for Cold Love

The foundations for Cold Love may have been established very early on within our childhood. From birth and as we grow older, we consistently take-on additional information that modes interpretations and beliefs. Information that either corrects our previously flawed observations or further degrades our understanding of all things. No matter what term is used, data, information or input, these are presenting stimuli to our mental programming and constitute the basis for our perceptions.

Within the psychological arena, a mental stimulus is defined as the mental process of knowing, including aspects such as awareness, perception, reasoning, and judgment. That which comes to be known, as through perception, reasoning, or intuition.

It may be true that such mental stimulus presents knowledge, but who is to say that our knowledge can't be flawed. As we are exposed to certain stimuli our minds will be attempting to piece together a response that is consistent with our foundation of knowledge, that which is deep-seated into our subconsciousness by our past thoughts and experiences. Our heritage of what is true concerning most things and what matters most to us is an interpretation of the combined knowledge of what was passed on to us and then acquired through experience.

Before our current time, it could take Scientists perhaps hundreds of years to correct bad teachings or misunderstood information. In our lifetime, we now see Science making major breakthroughs in numerous areas, correcting older errors in only a few years. Those Science or History books we used in High School just a few decades back most likely contained information that has since been corrected or greatly expanded. All information passed onto us builds our foundation of knowledge.

The sum of our storeroom of knowledge consists of a combination of what we were taught and our life's experiences combined. Keep in mind that we are constantly making interpretations of our own experiences based on what we understand to be true at that specific time. If we hope to dampen the effects that Cold Love may be playing in our lives, then we must attempt to update or change our inner beliefs, our foundation, in order to have a better chance at reacting to life's stimuli differently than before.

At some very young age, our parents may have allowed us to play with pots and pans. We then learned to associate the shiny metal objects as something that we could make lots of noise with. Then latter our association with these objects may have put us in grave danger as we reached to pull one of them off of the stove to play with. At that point, you either learned what a very hot material could do to your skin or perhaps you were caught in time and only received a scolding and warning. Can you still remember how confused you were? Your interpretation of the situation at that time was very dangerous and wrongful, and you had to develop a more-true understanding of when you could play with the pots and pans, right!

Why is it that when we are very young, a light slapping of someone's face is seen as lovable and playful. Then as we grow older, these actions most often got you into trouble. Try to consider the chaos that plays out in the mind of a child as they develop through the many barriers of right and wrong, dos and don'ts. How can a child make the proper associations when something is right one day, then wrong the next?

How many stories have you heard about someone growing up in an abusive family? Almost in every account, they become an abuser themselves, at least to some degree. Even if an abusive person knows in their own heart that what they are doing is wrong, they may still abuse others, and themselves. It is as if they have been through some form of brainwashing, or a forcible indoctrination to induce them to give up their basic beliefs or gut feelings. Then we have to ask ourselves; "what has occurred in this person's life to cause them to act in such a manner?". The greater question would be, "how can we prevent them from hurting others?", or, what can we do to diminish the abusive effects in our own lives?

Let us examine for a moment how information is stored in, or retrieved from, our brain cells. Some have studied and learned that information is chemically stored within the neurons that make up our brain matter. When our sensors detect certain stimuli, a change in our cell's RNA (ribonucleic acid) molecules occurs. Since RNA molecules play an important role in cell's synthesis of proteins, it is believed that memories are stored in "coded" proteins. My assertion is that the encoded information is stored with different levels of severity, or hierarchy, depending upon the intensity of the initial stimuli.

Let us say that you were exposed to abusive behavior for many years of your life. Now, you seek a reasonable way to prevent any form of abuse to occur or from being passed on to your family or friends. A good place to start would be to concentrate on that area of the brain that represents your creative thinking, or the right-brain hemisphere, while also understanding that the left-brain hemisphere must play a part in our logical thinking. Creative thinking differs from routine learning in that it goes far beyond the mere understanding of a problem or a condition perceived by the sensory organs.

Creative thinking is a tool that we can use to search through our backlog of prior learning experiences. We can use this tool to reorganize these impressions into new and differing patterns of thought. A reprogramming of ourselves is possible.

Correcting the stored information that is considered to be improper is not a quick or easy task to complete. It demands our focus and dedication to the effort. Dedication in that numerous consistent attempts may be required over time with a clear focus on that which may have caused our misunderstandings.

Some research has shown that the degree of stimuli required to alter our inner programming must be equal to or greater than the initial stimuli which created the misinformation in order to override the mind's desire to retrieve the bad information, or a new perhaps lesser degree of stimuli needs to be presented over a longer period of time.

If the brain is subjected to information, or stimuli, of a traumatic nature, a person may not consciously know what caused the problem initially. Stimuli from highly stressful experiences, such as chronic childhood abuse, or chronic abusive behavior within a relationship, can be so traumatic that those memories can hide like a shadow in the brain and can't easily be accessed. This syndrome is also known as, "traumatic memory block". Before a person would have any chance of dealing with this type of issue, the root-cause must be exposed and brought forward. If left unchecked, these suppressed memories can cause debilitating psychological problems, i.e.; anxiety, depression, post-traumatic stress disorder or dissociative disorders. Our goal is to expose the effects that Cold Love has presented within our lives and take control of our actions.

To correct the undesired chemically coded information, our mind may require an intense or prolonged stimulus to overcome the chemical levels that stored the information initially. Our best hope is to have a true desire to change. We have to have a great desire to overcome our bad programming, and that same desire must be exercised continually.

Keeping in mind that most information stored in anyone's mind, under the conditions of abuse, most likely had an intense stimulus presentation. When an abused person is latter placed in some familiar abusive situation, they will very often react to the situation without thinking things through. While most abusive personalities are aware that what they are doing is wrong, they also feel that they are out of control. They reacted subconsciously rather than weighing out the results of their actions. If they had carefully thought out the current situation based on their previous experiences, with the will to react differently, the situation could have been diffused rather quickly, when we allow the conscious mind to play a part.

Can we now consider that our definition of love can be environment hereditarily influenced? Children that were raised in an abusive environment have ingrained into their subconscious that hurting someone is a form of expressing love for that person. Abused children may grow up and inadvertently enter into abusive relationships seeing this as more typical, and thereby subconsciously create an abusive environment for themselves. They are expressing their need to seek out that which is most familiar to them. This is their understanding of what loving someone is all about. Without this familiarity, they feel that they are not being loved. Their interpretation of their situation is jaded. This is Cold Love, that darkened version of emotions which is misunderstood as being true love.

When we speak of, "The Foundations of Cold Love", we must accept all factors of our life, both past, and present. We must also believe that we may not be right all of the time, as we are expressing our interpretation of Love based on our understandings as a whole. Others' viewpoints must be weighted, evaluated and considered. Although we may never totally understand why some seem to enjoy hurting others unremorsefully, we can gain a greater understanding of what real love can bring into our lives, and how destructive Cold Love can be. Hoping to change others may present a futile mission, but allowing our understanding, and insight into a different aspect of how people express what they feel as Love, can be very enriching to both you and the people you choose to care about.

Chapter 25: Truth or Moral Credentialing

What we say to others is sometimes as vague as what is presented to us. How do we cull-out what is truth? Why is it that within a discussion, we often sense that the whole truth may not be present? Within this search for truth, while evaluating all known to us, that not all of the pieces of the puzzle fit together, it does not make sense to your reasoning.

How many times in our lives have we been presented with a person's account of a situation that we knew in our heart was bull-crap. Just someone trying to convince you that things are not as they appear to be. You want to believe, but you have been wrong to trust this person in the past. You don't want to be confrontational, but you don't want to be used or manipulated either. How do maintain our sense of balance, what is most important to us? Do we accept the half-truths and maintain some degree of the relationship, or demand honesty and risk losing any chance of maintaining the connection?

How does it make you feel when you ask someone a straight up question about something troubling you, then all you get in return are lies or some other form of selfish rationalization from them? You can feel inside that they are not being truthful, and even further troubling to you is how they can look you straight in the eyes while whitewashing the facts, and with a straight face the entire time. They attempt to make you feel as if you are the person who is misunderstanding the situation, turning each work spoken against you. Exasperating, right! The Psychological term for this type of manipulative behavior is; Moral Credentialing.

Cold Love would struggle to exist without the moral credentialing that occurs when people attempt to rationalize their misconduct. True that Cold Love likely played a part in the misconduct initially, but the attempt to rationalize the bad behavior only exacerbates the issues at hand and allows Cold Love to thrive. An area which seems to ignite moral credentialing most often in our society is the numerous and deliberate forms of cheating.

Moral Credentialing is often used by those who find themselves within a moral dilemma, as they use this form of mental manipulation in an attempt to vindicate themselves from an action. Often because they either wish to pursue the act or an attempt to justify a questionable act already performed.
Studies have shown that moral credentialing can allow a person to behave according to their "darker" impulses, the effort seemingly relieving them of any semblance of self-restraint often imposed by a socially tuned conscience. Through this form of self-manipulation, they establish themselves as a virtuous and moral person while facilitating selfish or ethically questionable behavior, whether the act of credentialing occurs in public or in private and whether it involves real or merely wish-filled behavior.

Moral Credentialing appears perplexing to psychological studies, as people in general have a strong motivation for self-consistency, and any violation of the consistency motive should be aversive to them. From a self-consistency perspective, a person wants to establish their moral credentials, yet this action should inhibit immoral behavior, not turn into a justification process. Given the consistency-based motive to reduce immoral behavior following the assertion of one's moral integrity, why would moral credentialing ever facilitate questionable misbehavior? The answer to this question can best be understood by broaching the topic of "rationalization".

Rationalization is simply a form of mental maneuvering. Rationalization can allow a person to be blinded to the harm they may cause others, to dampen their morality. Once this ethical barrier is breached, a person will self-enable immoral behavior, and allow their actions to be reinterpreted as moral. This form of Cold Love allows a person to erect a psychological barrier between their misbehavior and their ethical perceptions, enabling them to see themselves as "decent human beings" while they engage in immoral or unethical behavior. Thereby, the moral credentialing or rationalization can free a person to misbehave without being plagued by the disharmony and guilt that would otherwise be felt from their contradicting of their moral values. Rationalization is a desensitizing displacement of responsibility, a falsifying selfish action, a shifting of one's decision-making principles to suit their preferred conclusions while also protecting the self-concept from any undesirable repercussions. Call it moral credentialing or Rationalization, the deception is the same.

What is this place inside us that holds the truth? Truth not only of others, but as well of ourselves. When it comes right down to it, we are all individuals to this world. We are the only person who has experienced life as we have known it, and we alone possess our specific experiences and knowledge, and we base our decisions on our wealth of knowledge, not necessarily by what others believe to be true. We must know and understand that which is so unique. We often place so much importance in trying to understand others, but if as much effort was placed trying to know ourselves, then a greater understanding of others would follow.

Chapter 26: Cold Love Seeds Resentment

If we want to change the outcome of our future interactions, then the subject of Cold Love must be explored. We must understand the cause and effects. If Cold Love dwells inside us, then we must understand why. Where did it come from? What effect has it had on our lives? We can feel it's destructive power when someone treats us harshly? What long term effects will it have on our lives? Within these interactions, is there something being seeded inside of us that will cause us to treat ourselves or others harshly?

What I ask of you is to look deep inside your psyche. Let the hurt express itself without harsh self-judgement. The purpose is not to condemn, but to reconcile. Talk to your inner-self, showing compassion. Allow no outside influencing to direct your thoughts at this time, as we are seeking our innermost truth not other's opinion. If you have felt mistreated by someone, then find a way to relinquish the inner suffering, find a more positive perception. Forgiveness goes a long way in healing of the heart, and allows our resentment to wane. Resentment against ourselves which we may not have realized exist.

Resentment is that strong and painful bitterness presented within our understanding, caused when someone does something wrong to us. Resentment may not have an actual physical weight, but it can be a heavy burden to carry this unwanted mental baggage. Baggage that can linger for years if not confronted and resolved. Being hurt by Cold Love may have caused this resentment initially, but allowing it to become a part of who we are should not be acceptable.

Allowing resentment to taint our thoughts is allowing Cold Love to exist inside us.

Resentment can also be defined as an inner-anger or indignation, seeded as a result of Cold Love's treatment from others. Feelings of resentment is a much more common emotion than most individuals realize, or want admit. Those who experience resentment may have feelings of annoyance and shame and may often harbor a desire for retaliation or revenge. A person experiencing resentment may feel personally victimized and will often feel too angry or ashamed to openly discuss the resultant emotions, instead allowing the grudge to fester and later becomes expressed in the form of anger. In these instances, Cold Love becomes both the cause and effect.

Perhaps we have all lived in a self-induced hell of some measure, at one time or another. It doesn't matter who caused the hurt, everyone may suffer for it. We may not have been at fault, but we still permit the mental mutilation. Regardless of which side of the fault we dwell, we have to understand the consequences of our interactions, and how our reactions are molding our lives and our subconscious reactions to other stimuli.

Resentment can be caused by unresolved mental pain in a relationship and often due to the unwillingness or inability of a person to forgive. For reasons beyond the psychological sciences ability to resolve, we most often choose to harbor this unwanted inner-pain, holding onto these resentments until it destroys our relationships and eventually that part of us that we once valued. Within a relationship and a marriage specifically, these negative feelings and ongoing offences lead to intimacy withdrawal and a lack of compassion for the other. This mental pulling away will further progress the feelings of anger, sadness or disappointment, creating a malicious circle feeding off of itself. Some have described these feelings as being like a "sulfuric acid of contempt", as it begins to erode and eventually destroy their relationship. Once this level of disdain is reached, a person may not care who or what is left in the aftermath.

Feelings of resentment are not necessarily linked to any specific mental condition, but it is known that resentment can become the result of not expressing, or confronting, your emotions soon after the painful emotional experience. These dreadful emotions can arise from a true, imagined, or even a misunderstood statement or situation. Perhaps a single careless and insensitive comment from a friend or colleague which you felt was undeserving set your begrudging emotions into action against them.

Resentment can be felt toward a single individual or broadly applied to large groups of people, often with severe consequences. Forms of deep-seeded resentment may manifest into actions of racism or present a self-righteous persecution of another's religious beliefs, those of a measure in which wars have been waged. In all of these cases, the innocent suffers the most.

The everyday signs of resentment are not always easily perceived or recognized, and many forms exist. The following are just a few;
- Recurrent feelings or strong emotions of anger when thinking about a specific interaction.

- Inability to stop thinking about the experience that triggered the strong negative emotions.
- Feelings of regret, avoidance of conflict, and tension within a relationship.
- Feeling inadequate, that others place no value on you.
- Development of an altered perception of reality and finding it difficult to see any positive outcomes.

Resentment within intimate long-term relationships are not uncommon and can build-up over time to unhealthy levels if not addressed early on. Below are some of the root-causes found within our studies;
- When couples start to keep score, or one person feels that they are constantly having to do all of the housework, childcare, being the primary monetary provider, or even having to always initiate the emotional or intimate connection.
- When there appears to be an unbalanced power dynamic. When one partner feels consistently overpowered, bossed around, or unheard and undervalued.
- When there exist medical or health issues, one person may need to take-on the role of caregiver which can cause some feelings of resentment, especially if their own needs are not being met.

- When couples fail to communicate, especially when something is said or done that is perceived as hurtful to the other.

If resentment is left to fester under the surface, it can eventually grow in magnitude and eventually end the once valued relationships. Any couple who feels resentful towards their mate may find that talking about what's bothering them at the time of occurrence, no matter how trivial the issue may seem at the time, can reduce or even eliminate the level of resentment felt and most often will strengthen their connection.

Resentment can be fleeting, diffusing quickly if the offense is realized as a simple misunderstanding, or an apology was accepted. Conversely, resentment can become a persistent emotion, causing a person to hold on to the negative feelings, revisiting the distressing event again and again until one becomes unable to let go of the anger or desire for revenge. If allowed to progress to this level, an individual's mental health is put at risk.

Resentment can also present an intoxicating effect within a person's life, as the feelings of anger and rage may give a false sense of power and seldom encourages a healthy form of expression of true emotions. This form of intoxication can become dangerous, as any intoxication can, when these feelings of resentment grow unchecked and eventually manifest into hatred.

In an effort to prevent Cold Love from seeding resentment into your life, try to discuss your concerns with those you care to keep in your life. Discussing the mistakes known to you should not be viewed as a sign of weakness. Too often people think that by talking about their issues it makes them appear to be weak to others, but studies have shown that by expressing one's vulnerability you are then viewed as more approachable and more acceptable to others, far more than when they try to appear as picture-perfect. If others think of you as being faultless, then they feel inferior in telling you about their feelings of inadequacies. Open communication cannot exist if we fear discussion with others.

Most of the time when we listen to others, we don't always take what is said at face value. We listen, yet we also pick-up clues from what we sense they are trying to express. During these discussions, a person may feel as if they are being attacked, or that their beliefs are being questioned. Some may even feel as if your taking sides against them. Try not to be defensive or judgmental, just open up and express your true feelings. Studies have shown that the majority of people must be guided into deep conversation, as so many prefer shallow conservation in an attempt to mask their true emotions. Perhaps a result of the world we now live in where open communication and expression is not always encouraged.

Any person that has gone through any form of separation or divorce in their lifetime has felt the pain of tearing away, a sort of reverse of loving passion! Having someone to talk with, to openly confide in, can be especially beneficial in these times. Confront the resentment in the early stages, before it reaches a boiling point. Be open to these discussions. Be that friend you wish someone had been to you. Ask the question; "is there something that you would like to discuss with me"? Now is your chance to help others and hopefully gain a greater understanding of that person, all while learning more about yourself.

Letting go of resentment is seldom easy to do, but there are measures to take that will assist you. Most importantly; stop ruminating on the past negatives! Stop rethinking the negative situations over and over to the point where you are reliving the past, not active in the present moment, not looking for a brighter future. The situation that harmed us and causing this resentment was, and still is, filled with negativity. As soon as your mind starts to reflect on the negative experience, turn your thoughts away from it, think of anything else, at least until you are ready to discuss with the offending person.

In most cases, letting go of resentment means having to forgive someone for their transgression. Even if it means letting go of the relationship, moving on, removing yourself from future exposure of Cold Love's effects. In the long run, it may be best for everyone involved. Regardless of what measures you take to rid your life of resentment, it must include the adjustment of your emotional state of mind, and how you interact with others. The effects of Cold Love may have seeded your resentment, but it's up to you to stop the self-victimization, or victim blaming. Questioning what you could have done to prevent the harmful past occurrence is only mentally healthy if your trying to learn from the past. Don't blame or continue to punish yourself, move on!

Chapter 27: Cold Love is Fickle

Perhaps we have all known that certain someone, that from one encounter to the next seemed as if they were a different person. One day they act as if they care a great deal for you, then suddenly, without provocation, they turn away from you. This situation is analogous to how many children treat their collection of numerous toys. You may have felt at times like that one specific and special toy. Being taken out to entertain someone's fleeting desires, but soon thrown aside and ignored until they themselves decide to spare us a few moments of their time, if not discarded altogether?

A *fickle* person will appear to have multiple personalities, and at times are in conflict even with themselves. The Cold Love *syndrome* includes immense mood swings which is a trait of being fickle. A fickle person, which is a carrier of Cold Love, is in such inner chaos that they themselves do not really understand what is going on, and they seldom concede to their actions. When others question them, they often take the position that they are being misunderstood. Even though shadowed, that is the only rationale that they confess to. It may not be so much that you are misunderstanding their own intentions, as much as their intentions are changing abruptly and they refuse to allow any form of focus or consistency. To some degree, they are prisoners of their own fleeting desires.

For hours you may plan a night out with this person. It all sounds so great. Later when the topic comes up again, they act as if no real plans were made. Cold Love's desires often last for only moments, days at the most. There is no question, Cold Love is Fickle!

The first few times that you go through this with this person, you may question your own sanity. You start to wonder what part of the conversation or situation you did not understand.

Fickle people are masters at rationalizing their viewpoint, hoping to vindicate their every action. Do not let this person's manipulations control your reasoning, as they will try to convince you that you totally misunderstood. Often these manipulations cause you to feel as if you have to start the relationship over again and again, and that you are so off-base that you become at a loss as to where to begin. The greatest wish of a fickle person is to have that clean plate, to start over. They often will leave a relationship if they feel as if they have been exposed or discovered. They know what they are doing, they just refuse to offer any form of true caring.

What is the benefit of having to start over again and again with this same person? Do we truly expect that they have learned from their past mistakes, or that they will change? What about you? Have you learned from those past interactions of being manipulated and used? How long can you mentally survive this type of interaction?

After trying to survive on this rollercoaster of emotions a few times over, you may again find yourself alone. What then? It is likely that you will find hesitation when trying to become involved with the next person that comes along. Who now suffers the most? You? The fickle person you were involved with before? It is more likely that it will be you and the next person that you attempt to become involved with, if you failed to understand the effects that Cold Love has left behind. You may have allowed the previous negative interactions to build barriers within your subconscious as you unknowingly present unbreachable walls to safeguard your psyche from further damage.

Going through such massive emotional swings with someone that you care about can cause severe emotive damage, to yourself and your future relationships. It may take a very loving and special person to pull you out of this inner conflict that has infested a part of your self-belief. However, finding that special person may be more difficult if you harbor resentment or hurt from the past. Being alone is a great option if that opportunity exists. Alone to work through the past pain and find your true purpose.

In order to better understand a person who is "fickle", we must explore the probable causes relating to these massive personality swings. In most cases, this person is allowing their personality to reflect how someone else has treated them, and their inner programming was flawed. No, I do not mean how you are treating them, how someone else that they may have had affections for treated them. A Cold Love provider will seldom rely on a singular interpretation of present conditions or base their analogy from the affections of a single source, although exceptions have been noted.

A fickle person is constantly seeking emotional nourishment from others. Yet they choose to flit from one relationship reality to another so that a foundation of refuge is never given an opportunity to mature. At times, it appears that being a responsible person is a very undesirable mission to them. They seldom see their personality as being self-destructive.

You will receive the better side of a fickle person's personality when others are not being so kind to them. They will turn away from any interaction which requires effort or a long-term commitment. Treating a fickle person kindly is regarded by them as an opportunity to feed their egos, a desired option.

Options to a Cold Love provider, a fickle person, is like giving them a shot of adrenaline. They now have self-proclaimed power to choose between more than one person or reality. They need this form of power to somehow prove their worth to themselves. If you are that option, allowing the deviant behavior, you will have their full attention for some duration, as they view you as the winner of their conceited offerings. Soon after, expect the old brush-off, as their impulsiveness rules their desires.

If you are involved with this type of person, and it seems as if you are getting the short end of the stick more than you desire, then you must find a way to protect yourself. Try to see yourself in a defensive position. You must open your eyes to the games that are being played on you. Exercise your will and emotional power over this person that is playing these manipulative games against you.

If you can get a grip on this situation and manage to rescue yourself, you will likely want to start seeing someone new. Be cautious! Fickle people are waiting out there, wanting to show you the attention you desire. They will lavish you with their kind words, even express sympathy for your past negative interactions, all while learning about what not to do that may tip you off or allow you to see their true intent. Be cautious not to fall back into your old habits. Opening up too quickly, or given all that you have without proof that they are deserving. Remember that you present a challenge to a fickle person, and they are accustomed to getting what they want. For those who dish out Cold Love, you have become a tempting target, a hill to climb.

At this point, it may sound as if I am suggesting that you play the same games as the Cold Love provider may exhibit. This is not what I am asserting. What I am asking of you, is to find a means of protecting yourself, not to fight fire with fire. What ground is won in this battle to find true love if we lose ourselves in the process?

Let me take a guess at your type of personality. You are a very kind and loving person. You probably wear your heart on your sleeve, or so you are told quite frequently. It is easy for you to show affection, and you fall in love easily with people that you are attracted to. You are willing to give everything of yourself if you could find that special person to treat you the same. You desire outer beauty, yet know that inner beauty is most valuable.

If you are this person having a special positive attitude toward life, just know that you are not alone. There are those out there that will love you for who you are. You must however realize that you are among the few, the minority. Your special person awaits you, as you each are hoping to connect. If you are ever to find the right person that can share in your life, in all of the right ways, you must show what you have to offer. The person that is right for you will not take your ways or remarks out of context. They will see you for what and who you truly are, and be not only understanding but glad to have found you at last.

Chapter 28: Cold Love Thrives in Narcissism

The term "Narcissism" was taken from stories told in Greek Mythology. There exist numerous versions of this story, told of the Laconian hunter who was the son of the river god Cephissus. His name was "Narcissus". These tales speak of a very handsome young man that many fell in love with. This wouldn't pose a problem if not for the fact that Narcissus held the vision of himself above all others. One version of the story tells of Narcissus, while on a hunting trip, became very thirsty. As he kneeled by a pool of water, he was captivated by his own reflection. Being so overcome with his own image of beauty and his desire to possess it, he refused to drink so as not to disturb the portrait, in fear of losing sight of it. The myth goes on to say that Narcissus refused to leave the pool and eventually dies of thirst.

A person being a Narcissist would not have the ability to show true love, nor appreciate its value. A Narcissist exhibits numerous degrees of Cold Love, utilizing the entire spectrum within their everyday interactions. There is no question as to what came first, Cold Love or Narcissism, as Cold Love is a consequence of Narcissism, and Cold Love thrives within. Cold Love can exist within many personality types, but a Narcissist is like the God Father of Cold Love's many personality disorders.

A person with a narcissistic personality possesses a dangerous level of self-importance, a strong sense of entitlement, and a deep need to be revered. They are most often envious of others, all while they demand that others envy them. They lack any degree of empathy for others and will say or do whatever they must to exploit what they want. Most people view a narcissist, rightfully so, as being self-absorbed, controlling, intolerant, selfish, and insensitive. If, or when, a narcissist feels they are not getting what they want, or they feel scorned or belittled, they have it in them to fly into a fit of destructive fury with a vengeance. This form of reaction is called a "narcissistic rage", and often has devastating consequences for all within their fallout zone.

Narcissism is classified as a personality disorder and must be understood by those hoping to shield themselves from future harm. We must understand the deep insecurities felt by a narcissistic person, and what lengths they will go to hide those shortcomings. In today's society, we use the term "narcissism" perhaps a bit too broadly to describe somebody who is arrogant, lavish, selfish, and even superficially charming. As a society, we have come to view narcissism on a spectrum scale, similar to how Cold Love is described within this publication. Perhaps there are acceptable degrees of narcissism, those which are benign and communally advantageous, those scenarios where Cold Love exists to a lesser degree. But, what about the more pathological types, the NPDs of the world?

A person having a Narcissistic Personality Disorder (NPD) presents a chronic syndrome of atypical behavior categorized as inflated feelings of self-importance, an excessive need for admiration, and a total lack of empathy. This form of Narcissists can never show true love, only Cold Love. Within each relationship they enter, they see it as a transaction, similar to how a shady business person hopes to sell something of little-to-no worth for a good price. A Narcissist is only looking to become close to someone for what they can get out of it. Depending on the situation, and timeframe, the Narcissist will eventually rob you of anything of monetary value, usurp your enthusiasm for life, destroy your self-esteem, and eventually abandon you with no regard to the damage they have left behind. You are a resource to them, nothing more.

A narcissist is a master at making Cold Love appear to be real love. A narcissist knows exactly what to say to manipulate your every belief, and to some degree, they may even believe what they are saying themselves. Their mind just isn't wired the same as those having sincerity in their hearts. Upon first encounter, we may view a narcissist as being a very slick-talker, overly-friendly, easy to connect with, outwardly bold and confident, even exciting and adventurous, but most often it is all a façade, the enticements of a master manipulator. Narcissists use other people who are typically highly empathic in order to satisfy their sense of self-worth, which makes them feel powerful. But, because of their low self-esteem, their egos can be hurt very easily, which increases their need for compliments.

Regardless of the negative traits possessed by a Narcissist, they do not always "love-them and leave-them". They can and often do enter into a marriage and have children if they see a long-term benefit for themselves, or they wish to strengthen their power-bond over another. Most often they will choose someone who is empathic, as they are often very soft-hearted and easier to manipulate.
Empaths are the opposite of narcissists. While people with a narcissistic personality disorder have no empathy and thrive on the need for admiration, empaths are highly sensitive and in tune with other people's emotions. Empaths are "emotional sponges," who can absorb feelings from other people very easily. But, what about the children?
Even with one parent being empathic, the narcissistic traits will always dominate the overall upbringing of the children. Children of a narcissist can, and most often will, take-on the narcissistic traits. The children will not be of a supporting nature to others, as they have observed the behavior of the dominate parent throughout their lives. The child quickly learns that manipulation and guilt are effective tactics in getting what they want, along with aggression and

intimidation to get their way in all things. As previously discussed, Narcissistic Personality Disorders (NPD) is considered to be a personality disorder or defect, and levels of this syndrome can be inherited both genetically and by contributing environmental factors, although the environmental inherited traits may not be as severe or chronic as the genetic condition.

Narcissists who are especially effective at winning the affection and praise of others may also leave a trail of broken relationships behind them once they've been found out. A narcissist wants new conquests to believe that it was he or she who had been the "victim" or the "wounded party" in any previous break-ups. They will lavishly embellish their own good qualities as they enthusiastically vilify their past partners.

Many professionals think of narcissism, like many other mental health issues, as being on a continuum. And while true that narcissistic people are certainly self-centered, can we conclude that self-centered people are narcissistic? No! Not necessarily. By definition, self-centered people are merely self-centered. People who were perhaps put on a pedestal as children and made to be the center of their parents' world, or perhaps didn't receive the necessary discipline or proper structure. Being self-centered is not the same as being narcissistic, but being self-centered can evolve into narcissistic behavior.

Symptoms of a Narcissist;
- Have an exaggerated sense of self-importance.
- Have a sense of entitlement and require constant excessive admiration.
- Expect to be recognized as superior even without achievements that warrant it.
- Exaggerate achievements and talents.

- Be preoccupied with fantasies of success, power, brilliance, beauty or the perfect mate.

Narcissists are preoccupied with the superficial aspects of life. Social status, a person's weight and physical beauty, all at the expense of committing to deeper values. They tend to indulge themselves by shopping a lot, getting mani-pedi's or spending a lot of time in the gym building muscle or toning their shapely body. They present well, but they don't necessarily play well with others. And if you think someone is a narcissist based on appearance, they probably are!

Narcissists are found throughout the world's population. Every city, township, and metro areas will have their share. They exist in various forms, exhibiting varying degrees of negative traits, ranging from somewhat caring to extremely lethal. They dominate our social media, the untold number of reality shows on TV, the corrupt political campaigns, and the vast world of entertaining music and movies. While a narcissist can be viewed as attractive, amusing, skilled, and humorous to watch from a distance, you may want to think twice before marrying one.

If you are already intertwined with one, you may already be living a life filled with misperception, uncertainty, and a damaged self-esteem. If not already involved, just know that the chances of hooking up with a narcissist at some point in your dating relationship lifetime is highly probable. It's often their physical appearance, their charming ways, or their ability to manipulate along with their laser-focused intent in getting what they want that eventually reels you in. They will enthusiastically romance you, sweep you off your feet. Taking you to nice places, saying everything you want or need to hear. Once their needs are met, they devour your spirit and spit you out, with no warning or justification. If you are beautiful or handsome, and somewhat insecure, a "giver" in a relationship, then you are a prime target to the Narcissist. If you want to avoid being taken in by their game-playing, the key is to recognize their methods, then steer away from them as quickly as possible. If your relationship has to end, caution must be taken that you don't provoke them into an uncontainable rage.

"Narcissistic Rage" is the uncontrollable and unexpected eruption of intense anger, often exhibited when a person with a narcissistic personality disorder feels that they are being challenged, or that their elevated self-worth is being threatened. A Narcissist will act and feel grandiose because they believe they are superior to all others. Questioning their motives or intentions instills a fear in them that they are not so omnipotent to you. That you see through their manipulation. If a disagreement breaks-out, try the steps below, if for no other reason than to protect yourself:

- Never try to convince a Narcissist that you are right and they are wrong.
- Try to empathize with their position, even if you don't agree.
- Use bonding language like, "We" and "Us", not separative words like "I" or "You".
- Never enter into an argument, or even a conversation, with a Narcissist, expecting an apology for their wrongdoing.
- Try changing the argument's root-cause topic to something you know interest them.
- Remember that a Narcissist is a master manipulator, and don't allow yourself to be baited.
- Remind yourself that you just want to get through this rage event, and it is unlikely that anything you say or do will change a Narcissist's viewpoint or opinions, there is no win-win.

Once the event has passed, there are other considerations that you will have to think through for yourself, especially if you are now contemplating a different form of relationship:
- Don't fall for the fantasy existence that the Narcissist wants you to believe in, make your own decisions as to what you want in life.
- Recognized that your needs and not being net and will never be fulfilled by this person.
- Take off the rose-colored glasses, as they have not served you well up to this point.
- Focus on your own dreams and what type of life you want to live.
- Make a plan that allows you to be a whole person and regain your self-respect.

You may have to keep reminding yourself that Narcissism is a sociopathic personality disorder exhibited by a person having a pattern of being self-centered, arrogant in their thinking and have aggressive behavior patterns, and that they lack any form of empathy or true consideration for other people. They have an excessive need for unwarranted admiration. They are cocky, manipulative, selfish, patronizing, and overly demanding. Narcissistic Rage is a sociopathic disorder manifesting itself in extreme antisocial attitudes and behavior with a lack of conscience.

Narcissism and Sociopaths exhibit similar profiles:
- Glibness and superficially charm.
- Manipulative and conning.
- They never recognize the rights of others and see their self-serving behaviors as permissible.
- Grandiose sense of themselves.
- Pathological liars.
- Exhibit total lack of remorse or guilt for their actions.
- Superficial desires and shallow emotions.

- Incapable of feeling or expressing true love.
- Have a constant desire for change and stimulation.

There exists a difference between a Narcissist and a Sociopath, in that a narcissist is somewhat unaware of their personality deficiency and how they affect others, while a Sociopath is likely to be aware that they are different and care nothing about the damage they cause. Neither are capable of experiencing or expressing empathy, and they both use whatever means necessary to get their way. A Sociopath is more likely to play-out his games over a longer period of time, while a Narcissist plays a shorter-term game.

The Diagnostic and Statistical Manual of Mental Disorders (DSM 5) lists Narcissistic Personality Disorder as a long-term mental health condition. This finding suggests that Narcissism, within the minor scale, can be viewed as socially healthy. At the minimal range, a Narcissist will exhibit traits like authority, willfulness, and self-sufficiency, which are beneficial if you're looking to climb the corporate ladder, become a rock star, or a professional athlete. On the higher-end or unhealthy range of the DSM 5 scale exist the traits like entitlement, exhibitionism, and exploitativeness, which can make it difficult to maintain close relationships over long periods. Entitlement means that you see yourself as deserving special treatment and extra privileges that others aren't afforded. Exhibitionism means you like to show off, often inappropriately, and Exploitativeness means that you use other people to advance your own goals or meet your own needs, rather than seeing people as intrinsically valuable. These traits may explain why people in relationships with narcissists often don't feel seen and respected.

Now that you understand more about what Cold Love and Narcissism presents, you are better informed about how to spot the warning signs and make a more informed decision of whether your partner or associate is a narcissist. They may appear seductive, exciting, intense, and at the same time be arrogant and dismissive. Don't play their games! It is so easy to get hooked on the adrenalin a narcissist provokes, but you will pay a heavy price for that rush. Even now knowing that narcissism is a heritable biological-behavioral condition, doesn't make it OK for them to treat you badly. Being a narcissist makes it very difficult, if not impossible, for them to be authentic and trustworthy partner for the long-term. If you sign-up to a relationship with a narcissist, knowingly so, then prepare yourself, as you will get what you're asking for.

Chapter 29: Cold Love Destroys Self-Esteem

We have discussed that when others present Cold Love to us it damages our relationships in some form or another. Let us now examine further how this external stimulus effects our self-esteem.

Within most philosophies around the world, regardless of cultural or religious beliefs, people associate having a good self-esteem with feeling confident, happy, and sure of their actions. This is all well and good, if our days were filled with encouraging people, positive interactions, and constructive teachings. I think we can all agree that this is not the reality of things. The stimuli presented into our lives will always be a mixture of positive and negative as we view and judge them to be.

Are all positives a good thing, and all negatives a bad thing? Not necessarily! Hasn't there been times in your life when you at first thought of something, or someone, as being good and a positive influence in your life, only to learn later that your initial judgement was skewed in reality or just wrong? Conversely, what about that time when your pre-judged that certain something, or someone, as being bad, then later it turned out to be a great life-lesson, or the person turned out to be one of your best friends? The lesson to be learned in this, is that we shouldn't allow life's positives or negatives to govern our self-worth, or to control our levels of self-esteem.

You may also find it interesting that research has shown that we learn more from our negative interactions than we do our positive experiences. Some negative types of interactions help to stabilize our social structure, while others promote change. Among the most common forms of social interaction are verbal exchange, competition in various forms, conflict of all types, cooperation with one or the masses, and the accommodation of others. These five types of interaction occur in civilizations throughout the entire world. Within each of these interactive types both positives and negatives can be found, and Cold Love plays its role in abundance.

Various levels of Cold Love exist everywhere, affecting the majority of the earth's population. We can't hide from the negative interactions, but if we are to continue this self-judgement and determination of our self-worth, then we must learn to accept all occurrences as valid. Our self-judgement can't be based on any one occurrence that is always subject to change. Maintaining a positive self-esteem begins with a commitment to work toward accepting all of our feelings, whether pleasant or painful.

It is totally within our rights that that we all want to be happy. But, is feeling sadness the beginning of the end? Will we not live another day to pursue our desires? We often try to dismiss our painful feelings, push them aside and hope they either go away or self-resolve, yet that seldom if ever happens. We privilege happiness and condemn sadness, all while knowing that happiness is often a short-term high. Rather than accepting the unhappiness, learning from the experience, we convict ourselves. We succumb to the depletion of our self-esteem and give up on our long-term sense of stability. As we privilege the positive feelings over the negative, we fundamentally allow injury to our self-esteem. By dismissing a hurtful emotional state, we are inadvertently telling our subconscious that we are not okay. Our conscious expressions are the most spontaneous outward demonstration of who we are, but these expressions are guided by our subconscious programming. By telling our subconscious that we are not okay, we unconsciously condemn our outward expressions. Being intent on hiding a negative experience will not prevent you from feeling bad about yourself.

In order to gain some margin of control over the effects that Cold Love presents, and to strengthen our self-esteem, we must take action and accept the following;

- Honor Your Feelings: A more positive self-esteem starts with accepting your feelings as they arise, no matter what they are. This commitment will ensure that our self-esteem remains stable and grounded. This doesn't mean that we need to hide or react hastily to our feelings, only that we have to be accepting of them. Our feelings should inform our actions, not dictate how we react to them. Honoring our feelings means to label them, then to be accepting. Allow yourself to feel, but accept that this is just another characteristic of being human. Our feelings deserve our attention, and perhaps should be shared with others, but try to do so in a positive manner. Speaking negatively about your feelings will reinforce the destructive components that initiated the harm.
- Take Control: When we reinforce that only positive interactions elevate our sense of self-esteem, we are subjecting our self-worth to the instabilities of our impulsive emotional state, that which we can't control. If we commit to the practice of grounding our level of self-esteem and accepting our frame of mind without harsh judgment then our overall levels of self-esteem will improve with time. We have the ability to alter our subconscious programming, and to improve our attitude on life. These changes may not occur overnight, as you may have years or decades of negative programming to overcome. The first step towards this journey of healing is to make the commitment and follow-through, even if only in

small steps at a time. You will soon feel the value in this effort.
- Setting Achievable Goals: Positive goal setting is very important to anyone wanting to improve their life. Positive goals present a better direction to follow that present a more optimistic future. However, our initial goals should be within our current reach, attainable within a short amount of time, and without having to make a major sacrifice. This journey should begin with that single step, not by attempting a giant leap. If we set our initial goal too high, that which is beyond our current abilities, then we run the risk of failure. True that failing is a risk we all have to take, especially when trying something new, but failing can also help to guide us, if we don't allow the negative self-condemnation. Inaction, or failing to try is the most damaging to our self-esteem. If you want to set a long-term larger goal, you should start by breaking it down into manageable obtainable steps. Just trying to acknowledge one negative feeling or thought each day is a step in the right direction. Take that one negative thought, label it, then accept that it's okay to have these feeling without condemning yourself.
- Remember: You must own your "Self-Esteem": It is imperative that we understand that our self-esteem is the measure of respect in which we hold ourselves to. It is not a quality or quantity in which others can award to us, nor a factor in which others are to judge us. Our measure of self-esteem should not be dependent upon how others treat us or allow us to feel. If we allow others to set our level of self-respect, then we will always be at their mercy and daily impulses. Why is it that when someone pays us a compliment, we feel good about ourselves? Then when something unkind is said, we condemn ourselves and feel terrible for days. It is natural to be

pleased to receive a compliment, or unhappy to hear harsh words, but these feelings should be accepted at what they are, as being someone else's momentary opinion, not your true value.

- Accepting Your Feelings = Valuing Yourself: If you find that you are struggling to accept your emotional state, there are measures you can take. Find a trustful friend to confide in, or seek professional help which many find beneficial. When we are exposed to Cold Love over long periods of time, in relationships, or within the family environment, we may find it difficult to value certain feelings. Exposer to negative stimuli can present mental blocks, harmful mental programming, and those unresolved issues can hamper our ability to function in a positive manner. Eventually, these unresolved issues will turn on us. As hurtful as some emotions can be, it is always worse to hide them, or somehow convince ourselves that we should not be feeling unhappy about them. When we ignore the unwanted emotion, we multiple it's negative impact, and it will soon damage our self-esteem.

Chapter 30: Falling Out of Love

Most shattered relationship couples will agree on how heartbroken they were to feel their once hope-filled desires deteriorate and eventually see the relationship totally fall apart. It's a tragic thing to live through, the "falling out of love" for someone we once valued so intensely. To feel the emptiness creeping in. That feelings of despair taking over our every moment of thought, haunting our dreams, draining us of our self-worth. How each person handles this process may set the tone for any future relationship that may come thereafter.

Like it or not, it's just a fact of life that not all dreams come true, or that all promises will be fulfilled, even when all of the early indicators are positive. People and circumstances change. Unforeseen events and situations alter the course of things to come. One can't expect to totally control the future, as we only have the ability to affect the outcome hopefully. We must all come to realize that we are not the same person as before, nor is our mate, as even with the slightest alteration of desires bring change to your interpretations of the present-day. As our wants, needs, and perceptions change, the distance and disconnects may build to the point where a separation is seen as the only viable option. Sort of a "we're just too different" type of situation, as you grow further and further apart.

Over the past several decades, numerous studies have been conducted in an attempt to answer the questions as to why the separation and divorce rates are increasing globally. The merged data considers relationships as a whole, as many couples are opting to cohabitate rather than committing to the more demanding aspects of a marriage. Overall, the statistics confirm that a high majority of all relationships will fail. These studies were not conducted in an attempt to determine who was more right or wrong, but did however present useful information on the "cause" or reasoning behind the failed relationship efforts.

Many of us are aware that the divorce rate in America has hovered around 50% for a few decades now, and the #1 problematic issue presented was "money problems". The consensus confirms that financial issues present a heavy emotional toll on couples, causing unresolved disputes that can debilitate a couple's ability to communicate effectively and eventually will devastate the family bond. Without this bond, intimacy may all but disappear from their interactions, and without intimacy Cold Love creeps in.

As previously discussed, couples most often come together because of the sexual attraction between them. That brain-chemical stimulus which causes an intimate primordial desire to bond closely. Sexual intimacy can be viewed as the glue that bonds people together, or the fuel that keeps the loving passion alive. Without this sexual interaction, and no other similar form of stimulus available, both love and the bond diminish.

People finding themselves in a sexless relationship often feel that this issue is unique to them, not being aware of the truth that surrounds them. Perhaps because most couples are hesitant to share these intimate facts with their friends or family, fearing that they will be viewed as inadequate or judged at fault. The facts revealed below, composed from the research data, may assist in your understanding that you are not alone.

In a study of over 26,000 Americans, the data is averaged* to reflect the following;
- 15% to 20% of couples are in a sexless relationship.

- 10% or less of the married population below age 50 have not had sex in the past year.
- Less than 20% report having sex only a few times per year, or even monthly, under the age 40.
- The 7th year of marriage is the most challenging for American couples. Also known as the 7-year itch.
- Younger couples living together report having sex 146* times per year.
- Young married couples report having sex 98* times per year.
- Singles report having sex the least at 49* times a year.

Understanding these facts, and knowing that you are not unique in this process of "falling out of love", may present some form of forgiveness to those of self-persecution. For as we forgo the sexual bonding, once spurred by loving passion, we are allowing intimate desires to fade, inadvertently opening the gates wide for Cold Love to enter and gain strength in poisoning our wishes for tomorrow. Most give in, or give up the fight to maintain what once was, leaving only separation from the present state of things as their last resort.

How many have resolved to the state of divorce to solve their discontent? Throughout recorded history, in nations across this planet, mankind has developed laws that allow its residents to divorce under certain conditions. The exception being for 'most' residence of the Philippines and within the ecclesiastical sovereign city-state of Vatican City, which have no procedure for allowing couples to divorce. However, persons of the Muslim faith within the Philippines still maintain a right to divorce. The divorce rate in Japan is considerably less than in the United States, but growing rapidly as the years pass. About one in three Japanese marriages now end in divorce, four times the rate recorded in the 1950s, and double the rate in the

1970s. It appears that as populations grow and countries advance in technology that our ability to love long-term, or maintain our once heart-felt commitments, appears to be diminishing. In summary, as mankind progresses, it appears that we are losing our humanity.

All relationships eventually face hurdles. It's to be expected when couples are spending so much time together and attempting to agree on most things. Financial issues come up that may present problems or concerns in the relationship, perhaps some that stretch the available resources beyond reason. In most cases, our station in life limits us, or our wisdom is deficient in how best to deal with the problems. If we as couples do not learn how to be more kind, be more patience, act in greater maturity, then we are sacrificing the opportunities to keep love alive and growing. Any couple who has managed to stay in love over time knows they must feed and nurture their relationship, no matter what threatens to drive it apart.

In most recorded cases, there was a period of mounting disharmony that preceded the breakup, those of which the partners either failed to recognize or refused to address openly. If efforts to resolve is not presented in a timely manner or confronted properly, the conflicts will build upon each other, happen more frequently, grow in intensity, and cause more harm. To a point where many feels that their entire life is spiraling out of control. While one partner may become overly guarded and begin pushing away, the other partner may be deteriorating into their own version of distressful reality. The recurrent arguments become a part of everyday life, anticipatory and ritualistic, eating away at the essence that the once love-filled parties relied upon. By the time the actual separation occurs, both parties are torn apart inside, mentally exhausted, and often begin placing blame on the other for their diminishing capacity to rebound.

Eventually, both parties become so wounded and disillusioned that they can't remember what they once treasured in one another.

There are times when the stressors that caused a breakup do not come from within the relationship itself. At least some portion of these relationships could have survived if not for the outside negative influencing, or by allowing factors to enter the conflict that neither partner opted to steer clear of. These forms of outside stimuli may present unexpected psychological pressure, and present conflicting interpretations that can overwhelm a person's capacity to clearly reflect on what is most important to them. The mental power of a relentless unwelcoming family is often damaging and greatly miscalculated. Some will seek out a prior relationship partner, as they are most often willing to listen, overlooking that they may have selfish intent on destroying your current relationship.

Most people cannot end a failed relationship amicably, though many have tried. At first, they present agreeable terms, as distancing themselves from the cause of their inner pain is helpful to some degree initially. Shortly thereafter, the pain from their loss starts to take over and maintaining the love once felt becomes more difficult. Many fail to realize that we should all strive to obtain that no-fault no-blame outcome, and not allow hurt and anger to destroy what was felt in that past beloved relationship. What good comes from turning against that caring we once felt within our heart? Are we trying to punish them, feeling as though they are not deserving? Perhaps they are not, but this should not justify or allow self-persecution. If we can leave the past relationship and still cherish the love once felt in the past then we increase our chances of finding love again. Harboring hurt, mental pain, even guilt, hampers our ability to feel love again, and may be viewed by others as weakness.

There are numerous issues that can occur within relationships, either presented from the past or occurring in the present. Even as a couple, each person will most often attempt to deal with these problems on their own, not as a unified effort, fearing too much may be known by the other. The history of the other, difference in personalities, diverse long-term goals, unequal levels of morality, all expressing their unique version of a singular reality that multiple parties need to be in agreement with. Perhaps at least one of the partners will bring past unresolved issues into the relationship, some evident, others masked. Past repressed pain left unresolved, that which doesn't emerge until the current relationship matures, or when a similar circumstance presents itself.

Matters relating to intimate physical desires are not always discussed or exposed within the early stages of a relationship, yet will soon surface. Having unequal intimate appetites can create performance problems, feelings of inadequacies, and fear of infidelity by the other. Each person may harbor their disappointment of the other, but the disillusionment will soon manifest into distress which further *exacerbates* the issue.

One area of study exposes a grave self-inflicting issue, when one party allows their old or unfinished relationship to come back to haunt them, allowing old wounds to open and take precedence over their current partner. Although not anticipated by either party, the couple soon find that they can't speak openly or listen authentically as they did before. Older known negative issues, once viewed only as a small fraction of the relationship concerns, added to new issues presented, start to build over time to a point that overwhelms what once positive experiences counteracted. Betrayals happen in a single second of misguided decision. Promises once thought sincere are but a distant whisper. Future dreams dissolve with no hope of returning.

There are also times when a couple can do all they can, giving all that they know how, yet failure is still at their doorstep. As the negative build, desperation sets in. Calm rational thought seems impossible. Couples soon turn on each other as regret, guilt, or blame starts to surface fueling the downward spiral. The "falling out of love" can occur within even the most seemingly committed partners. They give up on their core beliefs and allow themselves to fall prey to *cynicism*. Cold Love starts as a single seed, but nourished with suspicion, skepticism or guilt, it grows to destroy a once love-filled heart.

Most people have the mental capability to end a relationship without losing love or respect for the other partner, yet based on the statistics the majority of people choose not to. Like many aspects in life, to love is a choice. Parents try to pass-on the skills they were taught, but often fall short of what is required due to their upbringing. The guidance from Social Media and interactions with piers are more often filled with selfish or misguided intent. The people most influential in our life seldom exhibits examples that it is possible to love each other beyond a breakup or that separation doesn't have to be the precursor to permanent disconnect.

Not all separations end in total discontent for each other. There exist exceptions where people choose to feel grateful that they had the experience and carry some portion of the love and respect they once felt for one another with them forever. As the years pass, they continue to express pride in what they gained from the past relationship, determined to remain grateful for the blessings created, despite the final outcome. These cases are rare, but can you imagine how different our lives could be if we journeyed through it filled with love and respect, without Cold Love's destructive influencing?

Chapter 31: Love & Cold Love, Evolves

How we define Love or Cold Love is not the same for everyone, nor is it a constant to anyone. It's a self-described value placed on our emotions at a specific time within our lifespan. The cold hard truth is, both Love and Cold Love will evolve as we experience different forms of stimuli over the years.

We all have a definition of what love is, or what it should be. We may have even stronger feelings about what love is not. We have made these declarations and will stand firm against anyone not in agreement. But, what about weeks from now or a few years down the road? Will you feel so committed to what you once believed?

At any given or defining moment, we title our emotions based on our past experiences, our life's story. Our opinions are based on what has been imprinted into our subconscious mind. Our teachings come from all facets of life. Be it within the family environment, religious teachings, academics, acquaintances, and especially from a current or expired relationship.

Consider a relationship that ended badly. It shattered your heart, and the memories still linger. The recounting of the past mental or physical injury will mold your beliefs, dispelling what you once believed to be true. Our idea of relationships and what love is changes, as does our definition of such. The trick is to accept what happened and the feelings now present, not to hold onto the hurt and resentment, if you want the healing to begin.

The point is that our definition of love is not a constant. It will continue to change throughout our lifespan, taking on different forms, growing and evolving. There are times when our understanding and beliefs become fragmented into pieces and must be reassembled. The goal is to become whole again, with a more mature perspective on what love is and meant to be.

Our definitions of what love is, or is not, may appear to be absolute at any point in time, but in reality, they are not hardened as cement or unchangeable. With every additional life-encounter experienced, we are bombarded with additional stimuli. These influences may present new highs and lows, new experiences, and revelations about ourselves and others. What we once firmly believed love to be is reshaped. Our determination must guide that redesign to a higher purpose.

Perhaps this is the beauty of love, that there is no "one size fits all". No standard in which all is measured. Love should be specific to each individual wanting to experience the emotion. Our judgment on "what love is" stands as subjective as the definition of beauty itself. Recall the idiom that "beauty is in the eyes of the beholder"! Can we agree also that "love is in the heart of the beholder"?

Love is immeasurable, and constantly changing throughout our lives in some degree or another. Having a single definition for all to agree upon isn't possible. Love is a very personal interpretation of what it should be, how it is to be expressed, and what makes us happy. This interpretation is based purely on the life experiences that have shaped our beliefs, those that no other person has wholly encountered.

Let's imagine for a moment that our love is a heart-shaped container, with a specific volume. Within this shape, we pour our feelings from intimate experiences, and as a whole defines what love is. At times we feel secure that our love is safe and protected against harm, so strong and invincible. As we experience life and the changes that are imminent, we soon learn differently. As we fill this container with our firm beliefs, this can also limit us to new or different understandings. As relationships evolve, the exchange of intimacy may decline. People tend to grow apart if the once valued love grows cold, or when Cold Love presents itself. Once these changes occur, the new expressions do not appear to fit into our confined definition of what love is.

If you hope to enter into a new relationship in the future, you must remain open-minded in your evaluations of love, what it is, and what it is to become. Love most often arrives without an invitation and can be totally unexpected, and is seldom planned. Love can enter your life as if it has dropped out of nowhere. Love may not always be what you wanted it to look like, or thought it would look like. We must remain flexible if we hope to feel love again. It is perfectly acceptable to hold onto our current definitions of love, as long as we leave room for the unknowns, new experiences, allow life to work its magic and expand our understanding. It's within these moments, this space, that we expand our hearts volume, learn, grow, and continually redefine love. We have very few other options. Because the day our definitions of love stop evolving, love becomes elusive.

Through the many years of research and counseling of married couples and those having relationships, some interesting facts were compiled. Below is just a sampling of the findings;

- A long-term relationship was considered to be 10-years or more in duration.
- A relationship within its 5-year term seemed to be when most of the infidelity occurred.
- At approximately the 3-year mark, couples having issues agreed that their overall efforts had dampened, and that trying to find new ways to makes the

relationship work seemed less important to them. Those attempting to take action to resolve disputes without guidance, having a mediator or counselor, often found that the effort often led to confrontation.
- At the 2-year mark, all agreed that their definition of love appeared to have changed. Some found that they grew closer to their mate, while the majority felt more distant.
- A short-term relationship was viewed as 4-month, on an average.
- At about the 3-month mark, when many agreed that the honeymoon was over, their interpretation of intimacy and personal interactions started to present new challenges.

The overall consensus was that the definition of love can be confusing at times, as how we feel intimately can become blurry as we dissect the love experience. There are so many factors to consider, and with each new experience, additional challenges can arise. All parties agreed that their definition of love changed over time, as they experienced different forms of the love encounter.

Let us examine the term "falling in love" for a moment. When does the actual "love" occur? Before or after the fall? According to the research, there are three basic stages; lust, attraction, then love itself. Falling is the process, love is the end result. Most believe, emphatically, that they are in total control of who they fall in love with, and when. Let's examine this certainty of mankind's assertion.

Within each stage of the "falling in love" process, your brain chemistry is acting to control your thoughts and reasoning. Your brain's neurotransmitters and hormones are sending out specific chemicals throughout your body, and each chemical type is purposeful. Most often, the conscience mind has very little to say about what chemicals are released or when. Let's

examine the stages of "falling in love" and the chemical interactions further;
- Lust is driven primarily by the hormone "testosterone" in males, "estrogen" in females. Lust occurs in all species, in one form or another, and considered to be one of mankind's basic animalistic instincts to drive propagation. Lust is when you are physically attracted and drawn to the object of your affection, presenting a need to seduce or induce someone into engaging in sexual behavior. Many humans mistakenly think this stage is love, but lust is different than love in many ways. For a person experiencing Cold Love, lust may be all that is required.
- Attraction is the second stage. That point when you start to obsess about your desired-one and crave their presence. The point when your heart races and your energy levels increase to a point where it becomes difficult to eat or sleep. Along with the feelings of excitement, you may even get sweaty palms. You find yourself uncontrollably fantasizing about all the things you can explore and share with this person. These emotions are produced when three specific neuro-chemicals are being released that control and influence the physiology of the nervous system.
  - Dopamine: Increased levels of dopamine is linked to how much a person becomes motivated, seeks reward, and driving their goal-setting behavior, thus exhibiting the drive to pursue your loved one, and fantasizing about them when not in their company. Dopamine creates a sense of uniqueness, making your lover seem exciting and special, to the point where you want to shout-out to the world.

- o Norepinephrine: Responsible for the high a person feels. That extra surge of energy that accompanies the rapid heart rhythm, as well as the loss of appetite and desire for sleep. Makes the body feel energetic and alert, ready to concur the world.
- o Serotonin: Serotonin is a vital chemical within the human body. A neurotransmitter, found primarily in the brain and blood platelets, used to transmit messages between nerve cells. It is believed to help regulate mood and social behavior, appetite and digestion, sleep, memory, and sexual functioning. Strangely enough, the research is suggesting that the process of "falling in love" may be causing a form of obsessive-compulsive disorder (OCD). The initial clinical findings show that serotonin decreases at this stage of falling in love, and the lower serotonin transporter protein levels may be causing the obsessive behavior exhibited, the "I can't live without them" type of feeling.
- The final stage being addressed here is the "Love" itself. Love is not so easily defined as most would think. As a noun, it can be an intense feeling of deep affection or having a great desire and finding pleasure in something. As a verb, it can be a deep romantic feeling or a sexual attachment to someone. Love can be felt on many levels, including the less desirable forms of Cold Love. Love is a very subjective state-of-mind to define. Love is known as the most intense emotions that we, as humans, can experience, having a great diversity of feelings, mental states, and attitudes. Love presents such intense feelings, and with having no limits, it can be viewed as both constructive and destructive. To address "love" in the

physiological sense, we must understand what role the hormone "Oxytocin" plays in this process. Oxytocin is also known as the "love hormone". Released by the pituitary gland and triggered by specific emotional states. It is responsible for human behaviors, specifically those associated with a desired relationship, or special bonding, and often presenting a calming effect or a feeling of tranquility.

Within each of the stages described above, either Pure Love or Cold Love may exist. Both forms having many levels, or plains of existence, both believing it is rightful.

Closing

Throughout the many years of study, counseling sessions, and exhaustive research, I have found solace in what others have taught me. Be it a Professor, Friend or Clients, all having a special story to tell. Each having their own perspective on Love and Life, perhaps as unique as my own.

I would not advocate that Cold Love is something that can be conquered, but I can confirm that it is something that can be guarded against. If we want a better life, to love without being used by other's selfishness, then we have to better understand our self-worth, and make the effort to obtain our life goals. Getting more of what we want in life, means having to put more effort into achieving those goals. We must all understand that others may take from us only what we allow or freely give to them. We can and must control our own fate.

There are few things in life that are more enjoyable or rewarding than true love. Be it for a child, parent, or life partner, nothing is stronger or more bonding. If we allow Cold Love to influence our decision-making processes, then we are relenting our goal of achieving good things, forsaking our dreams. Make the commitment today! Be the You, you were meant to be.

Glossary

(Definitions provide herein are presented to clarify the denotation specific to the context in which the word or phrase is used.)

Admonishment: To caution, advise, or counsel against something.

Animosity: A feeling of strong dislike, ill will, or enmity that tends to display itself in action.

Appeasement: To bring to a state of peace, quiet, ease, calm, or contentment; pacify, sooth.

Apprehension: A term applied to a model of consciousness in which nothing is affirmed or denied. A state of uncertainty; the level of anxiety triggered by the real or anticipated communication act.

Archetype of Personalities: Viewed as a typical personality, character, action, or a situation, that seems to represent universal patterns of human behavior.

Atoned: To make amends or reparation, to become reconciled.

Cognizant: State of awareness; having knowledge, understanding, realization, perception.

Conceptual Dominion: The composition of perceptions which are used to form the bases of one's character or personality.

Corporeal Beings: Existing in bodily form; having material or physical form or substance which is visible and tangible; mortal human.

Culpability: The condition of blameworthiness; a state of guilt, responsibility, fault, liability, accountability.

Cynicism: An inclination to believe that people are motivated purely by self-interest.

Deliberation: The process of thoughtfully weighing out options, emphasizes the use of logic and reason as opposed to power-struggle, creativity, or dialog.

Demoralization: A decay of morality, objectively observable and inevitably precede the destruction of the host.

Derailing: The process of disruption from a favored direction or path.

Dominant Societal Psychological Attitude: A powerful and influencing way of thinking or feeling about someone or something, typically one that is reflected in a person's behavior toward society or social relations, a reflected mental and emotional state of a person's behavior.

Emotional Intelligence (E.I.): The ability to recognize and regulate your emotional state and react in a positive productive manner; ability for helping others to control their emotional state; emotional awareness; harnessed emotions within the process of thinking and problem solving.

Environmental Hereditation: An extensive area of study stating that a person's environmental learned behavior will present inheritable traits. Also known as "conditioning" that can permanently affect development and continue to influence personality, emotions, and behavior in adulthood.

Exacerbates: To make a problem, bad situation, or negative feeling, worsen.

Extrapolations:
To infer or estimate by extending or projecting known inform ation.

Fickle: Fickle comes from the Old English word "ficol", for deceitful. Fickle describes someone changing frequently, especially as regards to one's loyalties, interests, or affections. Fickle implies an underlying perversity as a cause for the lack of mental stability.

Genetically Inherent Traits: Inherited traits that are controlled by the genes passed on to a person from their parents and can be influenced by environmental stimuli; genetics can also pre-program us to be able to learn or adapt specific behaviors more easily.

Indemnified: To secure against liability for an action; to absolve a person from responsibility for damage or loss arising from a wrongdoing; the act of not being held liable for harm, loss, or damages.

Innate Knowledge: A concept or item of knowledge which is said to be universal to all humanity. Something people are born with rather than something learned through experience.

Interpersonal Interpretation: Relating to the resultant conclusion formed from past interaction between people as the action of explaining the meaning of something.

Interpolations: To alter or corrupt a conclusion by inserting information which may, or may not, be suitable; the insertion of something questionable into other known factors to draw a final conclusion.

Interpret: To give or provide the meaning of; to construe or understand in a particular way.

Malevolent: producing harm or evil; exhibiting ill will; having a harmful influence.

Mediating: To bring about a conclusion working with all known factors.

Mental Programming: The process by which our subconscious minds imprint information from outside stimuli such as hearing, sight, and what we experienced throughout our lives. This imprinted information, our programming, guides our conscious minds, acting to direct our actions, beliefs, and habits. A person's mental programming can contain both negative and positive forms of data, not knowing which is more true or false.

Metamorphosis: Spoken in the non-physical form, denotes the change that occurs when one allows their mental state to be altered greatly.

Moral Credentialing: A person's mental manipulation of others in an attempt to vindicate themselves from an action; the action of self-justification when one attempts to validate behavior, or an attitude, with logical reasoning. Often used to guise inappropriate conduct or deeds.

Paroxysm: Can be viewed as a severe attack, outburst, or a sudden increase in intensity of an emotional state, recurring periodically without reasoning.

Perversity: a psychoanalytic concept proposing the ability to gain sexual gratification outside socially normative sexual behaviors.

Predilections: The tendency to think favorably of something in particular; predisposition or a bias.

Propagation: Multiplication or increase, as by natural reproduction.

Quid-Pro-Quo: A favor or advantage granted or expected in return for something; something for something; mutual consideration.

Rationalizing: The attempt to explain or justify one's own, or another's, behavior or attitude, with logical plausible reasoning, even if not true or appropriate.

Satirical Wit; The masked comical expressions by a person meant as sarcastic, critical, and mocking of another. May also be viewed as passive aggressive behavior.

Self-righteous: The display of moral superiority derived from a sense that one's beliefs, actions, or affiliations, are of greater virtue than those of the average person.

Sentient: Having the capacity to feel, perceive, and experience subjectively, while being aware of your own existence.

Snap-judgment: The act or process of judging hastily; the forming of an opinion without consideration or deliberation.

Supraliminal Discipline: The inability to perceive stimulus or influence existing beyond our threshold of consciousness.

Syndrome: A pattern of psychological symptoms that tend to go together.

Temporal: Of or relating to the material world; worldly; lasting only for a time; not eternal.

The Laws of Cause and Effect: States that for every consequence there exists a specific and predictable cause and for every cause, or action, there exists a specific and predictable effect. More simplistically, this means that for everything that we currently have in our lives, good, bad, or indifferent, is an effect that is a result of a specific cause of action.

Wanderlust: A strong desire, at times irresistible, to move about without true course; an impulse or urge to cause change in location or personal situation.

White Knight Syndrome: Having a compulsive need to rescue and protect others from their problems; the tendency to rescue people in intimate relationships, often at the expense of one's well-being.

www.ingramcontent.com/pod-product-compliance
Lightning Source LLC
Chambersburg PA
CBHW071503040426
42444CB00008B/1472